THE
STRENGTHSPATH
PRINCIPLE

YOUR ROADMAP TO CAREER SUCCESS

A SUCCESSPATH SERIES BOOK
BY DALE COBB

WESTBOW
PRESS®
A DIVISION OF THOMAS NELSON
& ZONDERVAN

WestBow Press books may be ordered through booksellers or by contacting:

WestBow Press
A Division of Thomas Nelson & Zondervan
1663 Liberty Drive
Bloomington, IN 47403
www.westbowpress.com
1 (866) 928-1240

ISBN: 978-1-5127-4666-2 (sc)
ISBN: 978-1-5127-4667-9 (e)

Print information available on the last page.

WestBow Press rev. date: 07/12/2016

CONTENTS

DEDICATION

Thank you to my parents,
Allen and Frances Cobb
who always encouraged me
to pursue my dreams…

And to my beautiful wife and editor
Susy who stood by me when
that wasn't going so well.

PROLOGUE

I use the term *STRENGTHSPATH* to describe a place where you move in harmony with who you are, in alignment with your special assignment. It's a magical pathway where the things you love to do and the things you're good at, merge together. It's at this corridor connection that you maximize your contribution, meeting the needs of clients and colleagues in the marketplace.

Have you ever worked on a project or taken a class where everything just seemed to come together? Or have you ever been a project participant or student where everything you did was a constant struggle? I easily made A's in some subjects like English and History, while wrestling with others like Math and Science. I spent hours playing Baseball, a sport where my skills developed quickly. But I spent just as many hours playing Basketball, where my skill-level got stuck.

I grew up working my teen years in a family construction business. I worked hard, but I just couldn't seem to grasp structure. Framing or putting up walls was a complete mystery even though I was exposed to it regularly. The plastering, then paperhanging trades, were much easier to get my mind around, and that's where I ended up finding some entrepreneurial success in my twenties.

In my thirties, I had some success as an outside sales representative. I made thousands of cold calls, built relationships leading to repeat customers and made crisp sales presentations that allowed me to excel in a competitive environment. I was allowed to craft my job into a role that fit me well. Eventually that was enough to get me promoted to a sales trainer position and into sales management roles that fit even better.

What struck me in the training and management positions, were the unique approaches of the successful people I trained and managed. I witnessed many truly gifted salespeople in action. And I collaborated with many truly gifted sales managers and trainers. But they were all different. Each of them had figured out ways to succeed that were as unique as they were. Some were funny, some were intense and serious. Some were extroverted and some more introverted. Some were people oriented and some task oriented. Many were structured presenters whose presentations came off like a well orchestrated symphony. Others were improvisational, something like jazz.

Looking back, there were several underlying universal principles working in every kind of arena I participated in. I now call these *The SUCCESSPATH Principles*. But I also had to account for an incredible amount of uniqueness. Each of these successful people were building on a distinct individualized *STRENGTHSPATH*, whether they were aware of it or not.

In 2010, I worked with my Dad to co-found a very successful job search firm in Central California, an area that USA Today called the 5th hardest place to find work in America. In that very difficult environment, 88% of our program graduates found work in 10 days or less. I also worked for two years as the Career Services Coordinator in a Career College.

Both of these coaching experiences allowed me to talk with hundreds of people who had been in work that didn't fit them well. Some were preparing themselves for work that was sure to fit just as poorly as the work they were leaving. Most of the people I coached had no idea what they were really good at. They seemed to be completely disconnected from work they enjoyed. They had High School Diplomas, Four-Year Degrees and Graduate Degrees, sometimes from prestigious universities. But in most cases, no one had ever sat down and talked with them about their natural abilities, intense interests and what that might mean for a career direction.

There was an important research sidebar to my work experiences as well. I think many people are born with a question in their heart. Mine began to surface around age 14 and it never went away. Summed up, my question is simple, "What are the Secrets to Success?" Why do some people succeed at work, sports, relationships, parenting, health and fitness while others fail? Can anyone be successful? Can anyone be successful at anything? Is there a *Cliff Notes Guide to Success*?

By age 19, I was turning my car into a classroom, devouring recordings by *Success Movement* authors like Zig Ziglar, Brian Tracy, Stephen Covey, Tony Robbins and many others. I also built a significant library, voraciously consuming books by these authors. I was fascinated by psychology and studied the ideas of Abraham Maslow, Victor Frankl, Carl Rogers, Albert Ellis, Aaron Beck and Martin Seligman. I scoured biographies of successful business professionals, athletes and artists. I researched the concepts of career development professionals like Richard Bolles, Laurence G. Boldt and life/work design experts like Richard Leider. My journey also had a pivotal faith component that led me to spiritual thought leaders like Robert Schuller, Rick Warren, Bill Hybels, Andy Stanley, Ed Young and Erwin McManus. Each has a theology of gifting. I've visited their faith communities, read their books and attended their workshops and seminars.

Initially, I focused on the universal principles presented by the *Success Movement*. But in my mid-twenties, I read one book that caused me to pivot. It was written by Denis Waitley, a former Blue Angel jet pilot, turned psychologist and motivational speaker. In Waitley's book, he very briefly made reference to *The Johnson O'Connor Research Foundation* and Aptitude Testing they did there. He suggested that all parents have their children tested for aptitudes. The Waitley tip led to me picking up a copy of Margaret E. Broadley's book, *Your Natural Gifts,* which described the foundation's work. I still have that copy with Waitley's recommendation right on the cover – "...can change people's lives".

In 1992, Don O. Clifton and Paula Nelson released a book titled, *Soar With Your Strengths*. Like *Your Natural Gifts*, this book presented solid research, this time by the Gallup Organization, confronting the "Anyone Can Do Anything" ideas I was so gripped by. In retrospect, the concepts in the "Strengths Movement" actually aligned perfectly with all of my life experiences and observations.

It isn't that the *Success Movement* – "Anyone Can Do Anything" resources are wrong, they are just incomplete. Most of them were missing a critical piece. While a few mentioned natural talent, it clearly wasn't a focus that merited much explanation. Those individuals who already had the natural talent piece in place, even if they weren't aware of it, did very well.

Actually, there was a critical deception roaming freely, unchallenged in the Success Movement and it had crept into education. The belief that anyone, with a positive attitude and hard work can do anything is deceptive. It's still roaming freely in books, primarily focusing on "grit" while downplaying the "gift". Certainly grit is important. Even for those that discover their gifts, success requires hard work.

Most of our kids, employees, co-workers and bosses have been exposed to two damaging belief systems. The most damaging is the message, "You <u>Can't</u> Do Anything". This is tragic and still happens way too often at home and in educational settings. But the message, "You <u>Can</u> Do Anything" is also damaging. That damage is counter-intuitive and more subtle, but it's still damaging. It doesn't accurately explain the failures that most of us will encounter. And it leads to arrogance and ingratitude in those people who unknowingly fall into their gifting early. They truly don't understand why everyone can't do what they do. They often think, "anyone who's failing just needs to try a little harder".

This false, "You Can Do Anything" message is also a problem when it comes to assembling effective work teams. In this regard, sports coaches and music directors are way ahead of their corporate and educational counterparts when it comes to understanding the role of natural talent.

The truth about you is this – "You Can Do Amazing Things... When You Are Aligned With Your Natural Abilities!" But that's a very different message than, "You Can Do Anything".

Some of the success movement leaders are correcting the strengths message omission from earlier work. Stephen Covey's 8th Habit talks extensively about finding our unique voice. Jack Canfield, Tony Robbins and Brian Tracy have added a natural strengths message to their current work.

If you are interested in the Science behind the STRENGTHSPATH concept, I've opted to go light on that in this book. But from my research, there is overwhelming evidence behind what I'm presenting. I think I've done my homework. While there is still some open debate, much of what I'm presenting is based on solid evidence for personalized physiological and neurological responses. Our brains form neurons and millions of synapse connections. While our synapses can be reweighted, rewired and reconnected and our neurons can be regenerated well into old age, most of this happens before age 5 and completes by age 15. Lifelong neuroplasticity is very real. It also becomes more limited later in life.

My research has led me to study education leaders like Ken Robinson, Jenifer Fox and Harvard's Howard Gardner. Their ideas on multiple intelligence and learning theory has added new layers to my thinking. I've taken university coursework on differentiated learning strategies and looked into current research on so-called disabilities like dyslexia, autism and attention deficit disorder. Thomas Armstrong's book, *The Power of Neurodiversity* and Temple Grandin's *The Autistic Brain* have been amazingly instructive.

I think like a researcher and a reporter. I'm a careful observer, guinea pig and writer all rolled into one. I'm on a mission to find the truth about strengths oriented success and how each of us can experience more of it in healthy life-generating ways. I invite you to join me on the path.

CHAPTER 1

The STRENGTHSPATH Principle

Who This Book Is Written For

You are about to read something that could change your life forever! It's the book I wish I had been given 30 years ago.

This book is for anyone interested in becoming the **"Best Version of Themselves"**. It is designed to help you, **"Do Your Best, Doing What You Do Best"**. And it's for anyone actively involved in helping someone else discover, develop and deliver that **"Best Version Self"** as well.

I hope to make a special connection with those who are:

- **Shifting** - contemplating a career transition
- **Shaping** - crafting a job that partially fits
- **Succeeding** – striving to be world class in a job they love
- **Serving** – wanting to make a bigger contribution
- **Selecting** - a college major or first career
- **Stumbling – Struggling – Stuck** – with a career direction

I would also like to share these ideas with those who are:

- **Staffing** – attracting and hiring new team members
- **Supervising** – managing, training, teaching, educating, advising, counseling and especially those parenting

Given the current reports coming from the workplace, this message is deeply needed, even urgent. According to *The Washington Post*, only 27% of college graduates find work relating to their degree. And they've gone deeply in debt to get that degree.

Many of those who do connect with an employer, find that work frustrating and disconnected from their interests, natural talents and unique abilities. According to Gallup polls, less than 20% of employees report using their strengths on a daily basis. Research by Deloitte Consulting, Manpower Staffing and Franklin Covey, all conclude that large percentages of employees are deeply dissatisfied at work and looking for change.

Nicholas Lore has received accommodations from two U.S. Presidents for his work helping over 14,000 individuals make career transitions. Nick is the author of *The Pathfinder* and *What Now* co-authored with Anthony Spadafore. Nick estimates that 30% of employees see their work as a negative, to the point of being dysfunctional or disruptive. Another 10% actually may be dangerous.

This book is an introduction to *strengths-oriented* career development. It is intended to be a brief introduction for anyone interested in maximizing their professional success. I will lay out the case that all top achievers have figured out a way to leverage their unique *abilities* or what I call their *STRENGTHSPATH*. Strength is defined in various ways by different strengths strategists or practitioners. I define it this way:

A Strength is any resource, internal or external, that can be turned into a marketplace contribution.

In this book, we will be talking about eight internal resources, including passion, talent, personality, values, learning style, skills, knowledge and character.

The mother of all career and organizational development questions is, "What Leads To High Performance?" Or restated, "What Gets Results?"

I have spent much of my career considering that question. Most of my current waking hours are invested in thinking about how to help individuals discover their unique abilities, develop them into *strengths* and deliver stand out results in a marketplace role they love.

The right job, role or position can transform a person's life. It can even transform an entire family, possibly for generations. **The right person, in the right job, can transform a team, a business unit** and even an entire organization. I agree with Container Store CEO Kip Tindell who says, "**1 Great Person = 3 Good People**".

Zig Ziglar rightly inspired when he said, "We are designed for accomplishment, engineered for success, and endowed with the seeds of greatness."

I would add that we are:

Designed differently
Engineered uniquely

3

Endowed with seeds that bloom in varied colors, shades and hues

I do believe in, and regularly teach **"universal" success principles** that work for everyone with remarkable consistency. I believe in the importance of **Goal Setting, Positive Attitude, Leveraging Adversity, Team Work & Relationships, Leadership, Influence and Selling**. But the *STRENGTHSPATH* adds a missing piece. Success always has an architecture or structure. But that architecture is not only universal, it is cultural, contextual and individual as well. *STRENGTHSPATH* recognizes the universal, cultural and contextual elements of success while focusing on an understanding of **individual "uniqueness"**. A technique that works very well for one person, may not produce the same results for another. A strategy that works in Atlanta may not work in New York City.

A *STRENGTHSPATH* is a road, track or route that engages and utilizes the best of you. It is like an 8 lane super highway that allows you to set a direction, and then reach selected destinations easier and faster with greater efficiency and effectiveness.

Your *STRENGTHSPATH* has a strong neurological basis with a biological foundation. It is based on the idea of Super Highways or Pathways in the brain formed by synaptic connections between neurons or brain cells. Some of these connections are stronger and larger, while others are weaker and smaller. These connections are what create your unique abilities.

A *STRENGTHSPATH* is:

- A set of goals based on your gifts
- Achievement based on your aptitudes
- A purpose based on your passion
- A target based on your talent
- A quest based on your qualities and quirks
- A career based on your calling
- A job based on what jazzes you
- A vision based on your values
- "How You Rock" and '"How You Roll"

On these pages, I want to introduce you to ideas and methods that will get you started on your unique success-oriented path.

CHAPTER 2

Your Passion Path

The first *STRENGTHSPATH* dimension is what I call **PASSION**. Synonyms for passion are natural affinity, appetite, gusto, avidity, eagerness, fascination, intense interest, relish, delight, enthusiasm, excitement, energy, ambition, desire or simply, what you love. Your passion is a topic or task that draws you in. It's an activity or subject area that makes you feel strong.

The *Dictionary of Occupational Titles* lists over 13,000 potential occupations. Each of these represent a possible combination of subject areas and work activities. Here is a much briefer list to help you think about possibilities and passions. Whether you are reading this book to help select a college major or career, search for a job, shape an existing job, maximize your success or help someone else, think about ways to put together unique combinations that fit you.

Business
Administration, Entrepreneurship, Marketing, Sales, Retail, Real Estate, Restaurants, Advertising, Insurance, Manufacturing, Operations, Customer Service, Distribution, Transportation, Warehousing, Hospitality,

Statistics, Economics, Records, Accounting, Finance, Banking, Investments, Construction

Computing and Electronics
Engineering, Networking, Programing, Software, Hardware, Developing, Sales, Service, Internet, Gaming, Social Network, Data Base, Cell Phones, Computers, Television, Cameras, Music Players, Appliances

Education
Teaching, Adult Education, University, Junior College, Vocation, Early Childhood, Elementary, High School, Middle School, Corporate Training, Human Potential, Literacy, GED, Career Services, Counseling

Faith and Family
Ministries, Children, Youth, Hospitality, Small Groups, Bible Study, Evangelism, Serving, Spiritual Gifts, Church Plants, Missions, Teaching, Preaching, Parenting, Food, Cleaning, Child Care, Clothing, Shopping, Budgets, Decoration

Entertainment, Art, Culture and Sports
Architecture, Paintings, Photographs, Fashion, Interiors, Design, Sculpture, Flowers, Film, Dance, Music, Theater, Collections, Sports, Music, Festivals, Language, Writing, Speaking, Literature, Journalism, Library

Health, Healing and Helping
Medicine, Pharmaceuticals, Dental, Nursing, Laboratories, Radiology, Emergency, Fitness, Physical Therapy, Neurology, Counseling, Recovery, Social Work, Rehabilitation, Marriage/Family, Hunger, Children, Substance Abuse, Housing/Shelter, Elderly

Government, Law and Protection
Law, Court, Legislation, Labor Relations, Executive, Foreign Policy, Politics, Military, Fire Fighting, Police, Security, Investigation, Secret Service, Criminology

Did any of these topics stir something inside as you read them? Did any of the topics or tasks make you want to vigorously pump your fist and yell, "YES"?

Embedded in the word "Y.E.S.", we can find other clues.

<u>Y</u>earning – How do you feel **before** engaging a specific topic or task? For which topics and tasks do you yearn, even crave involvement? Which ones do you long for?

<u>E</u>ngaged – How do you feel **during** the engagement with this topic or task? Do you easily focus on it? Does it draw you in and then keep you there? Does time seem to fly by? Do you enjoy it? Does it energize you?

Mihaly Csikszentmihalyi (Chick-sent-me-high-ee) is a Hungarian immigrant and psychology professor who has spent much of his career investigating what he calls "Flow". **Flow is complete absorption**. In athletics, this flow state is often called "being in the zone". Jazz musicians refer to it as being "in the groove". It is a state of optimal productivity where an individual is fully immersed in what they are doing. In this state, you may lose all track of time.

<u>S</u>atisfaction – How do you feel **after** engagement with the topic or task? Some things leave us fulfilled afterward. They leave us with a warm afterglow. And then that fulfillment and satisfaction should lead back to the Yearning where we started. When that happens, you've built a victorious cycle.

I heard Oprah Winfrey share this insight, "Every single person who is super successful always says in some form that following your bliss or **following your passion is the way for you to be the most successful** and empowered person."

In her booklet, *What I Know For Sure*, Oprah writes, "Have the **courage** to follow your passion. If you don't know what your passion is, realize that one reason for your existence on earth is to find it. **Your life's work is to find your life's work and then exercise the discipline, tenacity and hard work it takes to pursue it.** <u>Ignoring your passion is like dying a slow death</u>. Your life is speaking to you every day, all the time and your job is to listen and find the clues. Passion whispers to you through your feelings, beckoning you toward your highest good. **Pay attention to what makes you feel energized, connected, stimulated - what gives you your juice**. Do what you love, **give it back in the form of service**, and you will do more than succeed. You will triumph."

Napoleon Hill said, "No one is richer than the person who has found their labor of love and is busily engaged in performing it."

After forty years of studying human potential, I have to agree.

Finding Your Mash Up

Road Trip Nation co-creator Nathan Gebhard talks about combining interests and passions. When doing high school presentations, he asks the students in the audience what they are interested in? He asks them to combine interests like art and writing, sports and science and then come up with an occupation. At one presentation, a student said, "I like walking and turtles. I want to be a turtle walker." So as part of the presentation, Nathan played a video, and behind the scenes had the staff *Google* "Turtle Walking". They literally found a woman who worked at a rehabilitation center for turtles. Within minutes they had the student up on stage, on the phone talking to a real-life turtle walker.

Growing up in the 1950's, Ed had two boyhood idols, Walt Disney and Albert Einstein. As he explains it, "Disney was all about inventing the new and Einstein was about explaining that which already was". Ed decided he wanted to be a Disney animator and pursued it. But it became clear his drawing wasn't good enough and the pathway to get there wasn't very well laid out. Ed decided to pursue his other love, science. He graduated with two degrees, one in physics and the other in a then emerging field called computer science.

Ed met a man who encouraged him to pursue an even more obscure subset of computer science. It was called computer graphics. All of a sudden, the other childhood dream was back in play. At age 26, Ed set a goal to develop a way to animate, not with pencil and paper, but using a computer. In 1972, he made his first short animated film. In 1986, he became the president of a new hardware company called Pixar Image Computer. Ed Catmull went on to co-found Pixar Animation collaborating with people like Steve Jobs and John Lassiter.

Several decades ago, leaders in the Success Movement were trying to teach people that passion or enthusiasm could be conjured up. In my Dale Carnegie training, we chanted, "To Be Enthusiastic, I Will Act Enthusiastic!" Success Motivation Institute founder, Paul J. Meyer taught us that we could increase our enthusiasm on a subject by studying it. The more we learned, the more enthusiasm we would generate. Both of these ideas have a measure of truth.

But consider what Jim Collins said in *Good to Great*, **"You can't manufacture passion or motivate people to**

feel passionate. You can only discover what ignites your passion and the passions of those around you.."

Amazon founder Jeff Bezos agrees, "**One of the huge mistakes people make is that they try to force an interest on themselves. You don't choose your passions; your passions choose you.**"

Working in your passion does not mean financial success will come quickly. Sometimes it takes many years. Working in your passion does not mean that success is not hard. Steve Jobs told us that it is exactly because success is so very hard that we need to discover our passion. Many believe passion is the pathway to an easy life. *Passion Test* author Janet Attwood addresses this, "Sometimes it's painful... Many people think that just because you live a passionate life you'll have no challenges, that once you know your passions it's like a smooth road, but it's not so. There are obstacles, there are challenges, there are moments when you go, 'I don't know whether to go right or left'."

Historically, passion incorporated the idea of sacrifice and suffering. I recommend watching *The Passion of the Christ* movie for the ultimate example of what I'm talking about. What is it that you love so much that you are willing to sacrifice and suffer for it?

More Thoughts on Passion

"My whole life, my whole spirit is to blow that horn, I've got to do it."
~Louis Armstrong, Jazz Musician

"I must write. It is a happiness I cannot sacrifice."
~Noah Webster, Composer of First American Dictionary

"I am a firm believer in the theory that people only do their best at things they truly enjoy. It is difficult to excel at something you don't enjoy."
~Jack Nicklaus, Golfing Great

"I love news. I love it. Cowboys dream of the herd. Journalists dream of the great story. I like to get up early. I like to stay late. I like to do news."
~Dan Rather, Journalist

"I wake up so excited I can't eat breakfast."
~Stephen Speilberg, Film Maker

"I am in love with music. I think of nothing but, and other things only when they make music more beautiful for me."
~Johannes Brahms, Composer 19th century

"I tap dance to work every morning. I get to do what I like to do every single day of the year."
~Warren Buffet, World's Greatest Investor

"When I do math problems I get goosebumps."
~Freeman Hrabowski, President of University of Maryland Baltimore County

"The only way to do great work is to love what you do. If you haven't found it yet, **keep looking**. Don't settle. As with all matters of the heart, you'll know it when you find it. Your time is limited; so don't waste it living someone else's life... Have the courage to follow your own heart and intuition. They somehow already know what you truly want to become. Everything else is secondary."
~Steve Jobs, Founder of Apple Computer

CHAPTER 3

Your Talent Path

The second critical dimension of a *STRENGTHSPATH* is **TALENT**. Inter-changeable concepts are aptitude, inborn ability, potential, gifting, knack, flair, bent, instinct, genius, inclination, brilliance and forte. Talent is what you are naturally good at. And as Lady Gaga sings, *Baby You Were Born This Way*. Talents are innate and enduring.

The late Gallup leader Don O. Clifton writes, "Talents naturally occur within you and cannot be acquired. They are inborn predispositions. They are things that you do instinctively."

Strengths Strategist Marcus Buckingham says, "Talent is a naturally recurring pattern of thought, feeling, or behavior that can be productively applied."

Bob McDonald and Don E. Hutcheson are founders of *The Highlands Program* and have developed a work sample assessment designed to identify inborn talent. They use this definition: "Natural talents and abilities are that inborn hardwiring that makes it easy to do some kinds of tasks and difficult to do others."

Rockport Institute founder and career coach Nicholas Lore writes on talent, "Everyone is born with a unique group of talents that are as individual as a fingerprint or snowflake.

These talents give each person a special ability to do certain kinds of tasks easily and happily, yet also make other tasks seem like pure torture. Can you imagine comedian Robin Williams trying to work as an accountant?"

Talents are inborn or innate. Talents are instinctual. Talents are natural. When you use a talent, you might experience what I call a **"made for this moment"**. You might get a sense that you were made or born to do that activity.

Using talents, like breathing, may seem almost effortless. At least it feels easy. That doesn't mean you don't need to work hard at a talent, but it might feel like you're not working as hard.

Rapid learning is a strong sign of talent. Results or success is a sign of talent.

Talents often show up early in life although there is frequently not an adult around who is paying attention.

Dilbert is a very successful comic strip written by Scott Adams. He regularly lampoons what's ridiculous about corporate America. A few years back, a TV cartoon series was developed based on the *Dilbert* character.

There is a great clip from one of the episodes circulating on YouTube that perfectly gives an example of what I'm talking about when I use the term "talent path". In the clip, Dilbert's mom takes him to the doctor with a concern about his habit of tearing mechanical devices apart around the house. He had just disassembled the television, a clock and a stereo and then used the components to build a ham radio set. (I hear stories like this all the time in my classes.)

The doctor shares with Dilbert's mom that he has a rare condition called *"The Knack"*. "The Knack", continues the doctor, "is a rare condition characterized by all things mechanical and electrical... and utter social ineptitude. He won't be able to lead a normal life... in fact he will be forced to become an engineer."

I'm convinced we all have "The Knack" although it may have absolutely nothing to do with mechanical aptitudes. Your "Knack" may be with music, marketing, ministry or any one of 10,000 other things.

Generically your knack will often include *Activity* Talents, *Aptitude* Talents and *Approach* Talents forming what I call the Talent Triangle. Again, whether you are reading this book to help select a college major or career, search for a job, shape an existing job, maximize your success or help someone else, think about ways to combine your talents and mix them with your passion.

Your Activity Talents

Your **Activity Talents** will often fall into **Four Types** or often a combination of type preferences.

The four include:

Working with People
Advise, Analyze, Build, Coach, Coordinate, Develop, Direct, Evaluate, Help, Inform, Inspire, Interview, Lead, Manage, Motivate, Observe, Organize, Persuade, Recruit, Rehabilitate, Research, Select, Serve, Sketch, Supervise, Teach, Test, Train, Unite

Working with Things

Adapt, Analyze, Arrange, Assemble, Balance, Budget, Build, Classify, Clean, Collect, Cook, Create, Deliver, Design, Diagnose, Display, Distribute, Drive, Estimate, Examine, Fix, Grow, Imagine, Improve, Inspect, Install, Invent, Inventory, Maintain, Operate, Paint, Photograph, Promote, Restore, Select, Sell, Sew, Set Up, Show, Sketch, Test, Weigh

Working with Ideas

Analyze, Arrange, Assemble, Brainstorm, Classify, Collect, Communicate, Connect, Create, Describe, Design, Develop, Discover, Display, Dramatize, Edit, Expand, Experiment, Express, File, Fix, Illustrate, Imagine, Implement, Improve, Improvise, Manage, Promote, Question, Recommend, Research, Sell, Shape, Share, Study, Summarize, Synergize, Systemize, Teach, Test

Working with Data or Information

Analyze, Arrange, Classify, Check, Collect, Communicate, Consolidate, Discover, Dissect, Edit, Explain, File, Illustrate, Interpret, Investigate, Log, Manage, Memorize, Organize, Protect, Question, Read, Research, Restore, Retrieve, Sell, Sort, Study, Summarize, Synthesize, Systemize, Test, Transcribe, Understand

That's a start, but you'll want to get even more granular in your self-awareness and which activities you are attracted to.

Your Aptitude Talents

Underneath these Activity Talents are Aptitudes. Harvard Professor, Howard Gardner has done extensive research with both Savants and those with brain injuries. Many in both categories have succeeded wildly, but often in very narrow niches. He concludes that there are ability specific regions of the brain, and therefore multiple intelligences or aptitudes in up to 9 areas. He suggests that most people have not one intelligence or set of aptitudes but a unique blend or hierarchy of several including:

Word Aptitudes
Number/Logic Aptitudes
Picture Aptitudes
Music Aptitudes
Body Aptitudes
People Aptitudes
Self Awareness Aptitudes
Nature Aptitudes
Existential Aptitudes

Gardner says we should not be asking, "How smart is this individual?" Rather we should be asking, "How is this individual smart?"

The Johnson O'Connor foundation grew out of aptitude and job fit research at General Electric. For career selection assessments it may be one of the most helpful. They use work sample tests, which tend to be the most accurate.

Johnson O'Connor accesses for 19 aptitudes including:

Personality – Preference for working in groups or alone
Graphoria – Clerical ability with figures and symbols
Ideaphoria – Fluency of ideas
Structural Visualization – Ability to think in 3 dimensions
Abstract Visualization – Ability to work with ideas
Inductive Reasoning – See connections in scattered facts
Analytical Reasoning – Separating into component parts
Finger Dexterity – Manipulating fingers skillfully
Tweezer Dexterity - Handling small tools easily

Observation – Taking careful notice
Design Memory – Memorizing designs rapidly
Tonal Memory – Remembering sounds and music notes
Pitch Discrimination – Differentiate musical tones
Rhythmic Ability – Ability to keep time
Timbre Discrimination – Detect sounds of same pitch & volume
Number Memory – Remembering numbers of all kinds
Proportional Appraisal – Discerning harmonious designs
Silograms – Ability to learn languages and technical jargon
Foresight – Look into the future with wisdom
Color Perception – Distinguish colors

The Johnson O'Connor Laboratory also measures eye dominance, physical energy, taste for sour and vocabulary.

Your Approach Talents

To explain the difference between Approach Talents and Activities or Aptitudes, let's consider comedians and crime fighters.

The job of a comedian or comic is to make people laugh. That is a talent or aptitude. But there are many approaches to that talent. Some of the approaches are related to a particular medium, but even within a single medium, there are many approaches.

You may make people laugh as a comedic actor, a comedy writer, a comic strip creator or a stand-up comedian. As a comic strip creator, you may have the gift for a single panel or multi-panel strip. You might have the ability to do both, but it's likely you'll be better at one or the other. And then consider the content and style of the strip. Could *Peanuts* creator Charles Schultz produce in the style of *Far Side* creator Gary Larson? I doubt it. Even within a single medium, their "Approaches" to comic strip humor are vastly different.

Consider "Approaches" to stand-up comedy. My favorite comedians include the quiet, slow talking Steven Wright and the zany maniacal Robin Williams. They both make me laugh. But their approaches to stand-up comedy are worlds apart. Make a list of 10 people that make you laugh. It's the same result, but not one of them will do it exactly the same way. Some are extremely gifted with physical comedy. That is, they use their body. With others, like Jim Carrey, it's facial expressions. Some tell a long story with a device called the "running gag". The late Johnny Carson had a way of getting laughs from his response to his jokes that didn't get laughs. When his topical humor sagged, he got funnier. Jerry Seinfeld's observational humor digs deeply into the minutia of everyday life.

What about crime fighters or super heroes? What makes them interesting isn't their crime fighting. What makes them interesting is how they do it. They all fight crime. Essentially they get the same results. The bad guys lose. But they all use a completely unique set of talents or powers. Superman, Batman, Green Hornet, Hulk, Spiderman, Wonder Woman and Thor are all very different in their approach. But each one has discovered, developed and delivers a set of strengths that are unique to them. And so should you. What's your super power?

If you would like a terrific assessment to help you identify your "Approach Talents", I recommend Gallup's *Strengthsfinder 2.0* which helps you identify a unique hierarchy of 34 Approaches to any activity. If 34 Approaches seems overwhelming, I recommend Marcus Buckingham's *StandOut 2.0*. This reduces the 34 Approaches down to 9, and is a little easier to get your mind around. You can purchase either of the books on my website and get a code to take the assessments.

More Thoughts on Talent

"I was wired at birth to allocate capital."
~ Warren Buffett, Investor

"I was terrible at running a design business, and I really wanted to just focus on the craft of design. I worked out what I was good at and what I was bad at. It became pretty clear what I wanted to do. I was really only interested in design. I was neither interested, or good at building a business."
~Jonathan Ive, Apple Design Team Leader

"I've learned to draw and read a little bit, but I'm really still a very one-sided person and I don't know a great deal. I have a limited intelligence and I use it in a particular direction."
~Richard Feynman, Nuclear Scientist, Nobel Prize Winner

"What makes some people more successful than others is their ability to have a clear vision of who they are and what talents they bring to the table. It helps people discover what I call the **"music inside of them"** and it's one of the most important elements in getting what you want in life and business. With clarity comes a sense of peace and calming, as you realize who you were meant to be and what you were meant to do."
~Brian Tracy, Author and Speaker

"People do best what comes naturally."
~John F. Kennedy, 35th U.S. President

"Success in the Knowledge Economy comes to those who do two things: identify and articulate their talents, and place themselves in a position to use them."
~Peter Drucker, Management Consultant

CHAPTER 4

Your Personality Path

Similar to your Approach Talent is a dimension of strength often referred to as **PERSONALITY** or temperament. Your personality is a crucial lane on your *STRENGTHSPATH*.

You might think of your personality style as a kind of map that suggests both your inner geography and the outward direction of your life. Whether you know it or not, to some extent, you follow its path every single day of your life.

We all spend a great deal of time assessing the personalities and temperaments of others. In a basic sense, it is simply getting to know, understand and then describe someone. As soon as we begin to describe a person, we generally use trait, temperament and personality language to do it.

People generally behave in patterned, organized and recognizable ways. If we say that someone is outgoing, we usually mean that they are outgoing with some degree of regularity. A pattern is implied. With some consistency, we can also say that some traits often come packaged together in a somewhat unique, yet similar and discernible grouping that we might call a personality type.

The evidence is strong that our personality comes from at least three places.

Nature - Your temperament is innate and natural from birth. These traits often show up as early as infancy and nearly always as toddlers.

Nurture - It is also influenced or shaped by your environment, family, culture and friends.

Choice - Your personality is a combined set of behaviors that can be selected and chosen at will. For example, I am naturally reserved, but I can choose to be gregarious and outgoing when the occasion calls for it.

Everyone seems to have patterns and natural preferences that can be observed.

Personalities can be described in terms of individual traits. Some personality psychologists explain them as a position on an axis or line between opposites. You can read through this list of trait examples and make a fairly accurate guess where you would be with regard to each set of traits. Are you more...

- Intense or Relaxed?
- Shy or Outgoing?
- Fast or Slow?
- Options-Open or Decisive?
- Analytical or Active?
- Independent or Dependent?
- Extroverted or Introverted?
- Driven or Care Free?
- Cheerful or Serious?

- Cautious or Adventurous?
- Leader or Follower?
- Flexible or Structured?
- Detailed or Global-Big Picture?
- Matching or Mismatching?
- Sequential or Random?
- Quantitative or Qualitative?
- Black & White or Continuum-Grey Scale?
- Competitive or Cooperative?
- Thinker or Feeler?
- Conceptual or Empirical?
- Task Oriented or People Oriented?
- Bold or Sensitive?

In some cases, you may have "Paradoxical Traits". You may possess, or at least have easy access to both traits at ends of a continuum. But in most cases, you will feel more comfortable operating on one side or the other. Working the other trait will be harder and feel more like work.

Often personality traits show up in groups. Those natural groupings have led to numerous sorting systems.

There are three different personality sorting systems that I have studied and use with clients. The three systems include:

- *D.I.S.C.*
- *Myers-Briggs*
- *Meta-Programs* from *Neuro-Linguistic Programming*

The Five-Factor or O.C.E.A.N. system is popular with many trained in psychology, but I don't use it because it includes a neurosis dimension that doesn't fit with what I do.

Never allow any assessment to define you with a declarative statement. But personality assessments can give you "hints" or "clues" that offer self-discovery insight. To maximize assessment results, make sure you customize the report. To do that, highlight the descriptions that describe you best. Have a partner or close friend read over the report and offer feedback. Re-write any inaccurate description so that it precisely portrays you. Realize that you can learn to "**play in all the rooms**". Some rooms will just be more comfortable.

The D.I.S.C. Profile

In this book, I only cover DISC. The DISC Profile is the most popular assessment used by organizations worldwide. Over 50 million people have used the instrument to communicate better and understand their talents and non-talents. DISC first came to prominence in the military - it was widely used as part of the US Army's recruitment process during the years leading to the Second World War. Having proved its value, it gradually came to be used in a business recruitment setting. Although the history goes all the way back to Hippocrates, around 500 B.C., the modern assessment was first developed by psychologist William Marsten who was a very interesting man. He was also the inventor of the lie-detector test and the super hero Wonder Woman. Marsten never attempted to copywrite the assessment, so today, slightly different versions are produced by different vendors.

DISC starts with only 4 basic behavior types, naturally grouping several dozen traits that commonly show up together.

Each letter in DISC represents a different trait grouping. The 4 types combine into thousands of possible patterns reflecting the complexity of human strengths. Sophisticated reports show up to 28 personality blends.

How I Use D.I.S.C.

- Suggest Potential Job Matches
- Identify Job Search Challenges
- Use In Building Interview Strategies
- Help Clients Become Comfortable Taking Assessments
- Training Salespeople and Leaders

D.I.S.C Style Overview

Direct
Direct
Directive
Doer
Determined
Decisive
Destination
Daring
Dominant
Driving
Problem Area-Demanding

Interactive
Interacting
Influencing
Inducing
Inspiring
Initiating
Inclusive
Instigating
Immediate
Inviting
Problem Area-Impulsive

Conceptual
Conceptual
Conscientious
Cautious
Calculating
Consistent
Classifying
Compliant
Contemplating
Controlled
Problem Area-Critical

Stabilizing
Stabilizing
Steadying
Sincere
Supporting
Standardizing
Sympathetic
Social Sameness
Sacrificial
Serving
Problem Area-Slow

It's not a perfect tool. **Everyone has a little of each style**. To get a quick sense of your own special blend, read each of the descriptors in the four categories and assign a number 1-10 (10 meaning very accurate) for how much the word describes you.

More Thoughts on Personality

"An elegant fit between you and your work includes and supports the full self-expression of your personality. Tell-tale signs of a career that doesn't fit your personality include: the necessity to assume a different personality at work, restricted self-expression, activities that conflict with your values."
-Nicholas Lore, Founder of Rockport Institute

"You are unique in the way that you navigate life. Every individual has his or her own personality, attitude, and way of being present day to day. Every individual has his or her own personal best way of being. Every person has their own best persona for generating results. **Your task is to discover and define your formula** and best persona for getting the most out of life. It will be unique to you, unlike anyone else's, and that's okay. It doesn't have to be commonsensical or mainstream conformist. If it works for you, based on results, then that's the test."
~Dr. Phil McGraw, Psychologist and TV Personality

"Most people are full of advice based on their own personal experience. Such advice should be received with caution. As you begin to recognize variations in personality, you also become aware that what works for one person won't necessarily work for another."
~Roger Birkman, Author of *True Colors*

"When I commanded the 2nd Brigade of the 101st Airborne Division, I had several gifted commanders with radically different personalities. I could tell one to go take a hill, and it was done. I could tell another to go take a hill and he

Dale Cobb

immediately asked questions: 'When? How? What other support can you give me? Do I have priority on resources? Then what do I do?' Both commanders would take the hill and accomplish the mission. Who was the better commander? The can-do commander was exciting and admirable, but he sometimes charged off without asking basic questions. He could get in trouble quickly. He did not always capture all my guidance and the larger picture of the battlefield. The other commander could annoy me with his pestering questions, but he often came up with a more skillful plan and more careful execution. My job was to get the best out of both and complement their strengths and shortcomings."
~Colin Powell, U.S. Secretary of State

CHAPTER 5

Your Values Path

VALUES are the next dimension that should be considered a part of your *STRENGTHSPATH*. Values are ideals, priorities, what's important to you, what you care about, what drives you and what motivates you. If you value a method, a person or an object, that means you appreciate, respect, prize, cherish or treasure them. Values, when they are aligned, form a culture.

In the book *ROADMAP*, Nathan Gebhard, Brian MacAllister and Mike Marriner talk about the difference between "Truths" and "Subjective Truths".

"Truths" include statements like:

Without water we die
Camels have three eyelids
Karaoke means "empty orchestra" in Japanese

"Subjective Truths" include:

I want to make a lot of money
I work best when I'm my own boss
I hate big cities

Values are subjective truths. Values may lead to standards, and they may often have moral consequences. But when I use the term, I don't mean it in the sense of morality and right or wrong. I cover that under another strength that I call character.

We all live by a very specific order, system or hierarchy of values. Other words for values are priorities or ideals. Countries have values. In America, our founding fathers held a clear set of values that shaped what we were to become. Some of those values included freedom, equality under the law, justice, choice, opportunity, representation, presumption of innocence, right to trial before a jury of peers, individuality, the pursuit of happiness. They were spelled out in documents like the Declaration of Independence, The Constitution and The Bill of Rights.

If you have a rule, a standard or an ideal, you will find a value behind it. When you use the word "should" there is almost always a value behind it. Families have values. Churches have values. Community service groups have values. Corporations have values. And individuals have values.

All companies have values with regard to things like product quality, speed, beauty, service, customer experience and pricing. In reality, they have these values in a sequence, hierarchy or order. No company or customer values them all equally.

Values came on the scene as a topic of serious study in 1914. German philosopher and psychologist Eduard Spranger published *Types of Men: the Psychology and Ethics of Personality*. Spranger described his research and observations concluding that six core values were found present in every person. He believed those values were what created drive and motivation.

An American Psychologist named Gordon Allport picked up on Spranger's work beginning in the 1950's. Allport believed that a person's personality type was connected to their values. I tend to agree with Allport on this and I would add that individual talent and passion is connected as well. For that reason, I believe that values have some biological or innate basis. In my thinking, values are less dynamic and not quite as influenced by environment or nurture as many would speculate.

In general, your values are a type of strength that should align with the organization you are working with. If you place a high value on customer experience and service but you work for an organization that doesn't, you won't be happy at work. The possible exception is if you are brought into an organization specifically to orchestrate a change in values. This is quite different than talent and personality strengths where a wide variety might be desirable. But with values, the organization is usually better off if everyone is on the same page (or a page nearby).

There are literally hundreds of potential values I could list. But I'm going to introduce this in a simple useable format.

Here is a list of values I often use as a starting point in my strengths clarification work.

I developed the acronym **M.Y. B.I.G. D.R.I.V.E.R.S.** as a memory aid.

Mastery - Growth, Development, Progress, Maturity
Yield - Money, Economic, Reward, Return, Compensation

Beauty – Aesthetics, Form, Artistic Expression
Influence – Authority, Control, Power
Giving – Service, Altruism, Helping

Discovery – Theory, Knowledge, Understanding, Truth
Regulatory – Structure, Order, Routine, Sameness
Individualistic - Independent, Uniqueness, Autonomy
Variety – Change, Newness, Innovation, Creativity
Excellence – Quality, Craftsmanship, Superiority
Relationships – Co-Workers, Collaboration, Team Work
Safety - Security, Protection, Caution, Guarantee

Some of these values may be important to you in one place or context but not in another. For example, beauty may be very important to you at home but only moderately important at work. So when you're trying to clarify your values, it's important that you think about a single context. A value may be universal but it also may be very specific to a particular environment. If you're considering this chapter with work in mind, make sure you are focusing on that context.

Also, this list of values may make you think of an important value that is not on the list. If that's the case, write it down. You may also think of a word that means the same as those listed, but for some reason your word has more power for you. Feel free to use your own words.

More Thoughts on Values

"All decision-making is a values clarifying exercise."
~Tony Robbins, Author and Speaker

"It's very important for people to know themselves and understand what their value system is, because if you don't know what your value system is, then you don't know what risks are worth taking and which ones are worth avoiding."
~Ben Carson, Surgeon

"A leader will find it difficult to articulate a coherent vision unless it expresses his core values, his basic identity...one must first embark on the formidable journey of self-discovery in order to create a vision with authentic soul."
~Mihaly Csikszentmihalyi, Psychologist, Author

"The founders of great, enduring organizations like Hewlett-Packard, 3M, and Johnson & Johnson often did not have a vision statement when they started out. They usually began with a set of strong personal core values and a relentless drive for progress and had—most importantly—a remarkable ability to translate these into concrete mechanisms...**You cannot "set" organizational values, you can only discover them. Nor can you "install" new core values into people. Core values are not something people "buy in" to. People must be predisposed to holding them.** Executives often ask me, 'How do we get people to share our core values?' You don't. Instead, the task is to *find* people who are already predisposed to sharing your core values. You must attract and then retain these people

and let those who aren't predisposed to sharing your core values go elsewhere."
~Jim Collins, Business Consultant, Author of *Good to Great*

"You have to decide what your priorities truly are – what it is that is truly important to you. What does success look like to you? What do you really stand for and where do you spend your time, energy and money? For example, among the things I value most in my life are my personal relationship with Jesus Christ; providing for, protecting and nurturing my family; my health; and being a responsible contributing member of society."
~Dr. Phil McGraw, Psychologist and TV Personality

CHAPTER 6

Your Learning Path

The next strengths dimension is your **LEARNING** path. This is your optimal way of learning. It includes your perception, organization, retention and response to instruction methods. It's a style or pattern of acquiring and processing information. Your learning path is the last of the innate or natural strengths covered in this book. The next chapter will move into the strengths that must be developed. Your unique learning style is the bridge.

My favorite story about learning styles comes from Dr. Ben Carson's book, *You Have A Brain*. During his first year in medical school, Dr. Carson went to class, studied and turned in his assignments. But he did so poorly on his exams that his faculty advisor called him in to offer some "helpful" advice. The advisor started out, "You seem to be an intelligent young man Mr. Carson. I'm sure there are many things you could do outside of medicine."

Those words devastated Ben and he decided to do some soul searching. This led to a vigorous analysis of how he'd managed to succeed academically in the past. He

39

wanted to discover what was missing in his current efforts. After serious thought, he became convinced that medical school wasn't set up to take advantage of his innate style of learning.

In medical school, he'd been sitting in lectures hour after hour every day. That was the pattern of each course, and as Ben describes it, "Nothing was sinking in". As he thought back over his previous academic successes, he realized he had never learned anything very well just from listening. He had always learned best by reading. Carson recalled, "That meant I had to come up with a way to use that strength."

The plan he came up with seemed drastic, and even as he says, "Crazy". Carson stopped attending class all together. While his classmates were attending lectures, he was in his room or the library reading and studying the course texts and resources. He paid a subscription for scribes, people who earned money attending lectures and taking notes. They provided a detailed set for every class and he added those to his reading time. Before the tests, the notes were transferred to flash cards for review. Additionally, he attended all labs for the hands-on experiments.

His strategy paid off immediately and shocked his med school advisor. If you don't know the rest of the story, Ben went on to become a leading pediatric neuro-surgeon. Leading a team of over 70, he was the first to successfully separate Siamese twins joined at the head. I recommend the movie *Gifted Hands*, with Cuba Gooding Jr. playing Dr. Carson.

One of the best little strengths books is *Managing Oneself*, by Peter Drucker. The section titled, *Am I a Reader or a Listener* is worth far more than the small price of the short book.

Drucker begins: "Far too few people even know that there are readers and listeners and that people are rarely both. Even fewer know which of the two they themselves are. But some examples will show how damaging such ignorance can be."

Drucker tells stories about presidents Franklin Roosevelt, Harry Truman, Dwight Eisenhower, John Kennedy and Lyndon Johnson. As he describes it:

Franklin Roosevelt was a listener
Harry Truman was listener
Dwight Eisenhower was a reader
John Kennedy was a reader
Lyndon Johnson was a listener

He describes the difficulties these presidents had when they tried to emulate a predecessor rather than stick with their own natural strengths. Press conferences went awry, elections were endangered and overall effectiveness was muted.

Dwight Eisenhower was a great reader and a poor listener. When he was Supreme Commander in Europe, he made sure that every question from the press was presented beforehand in writing. When working this way, Eisenhower was in complete command of his press conferences. When he became president, he stopped that successful strategy and tried to imitate Franklin Roosevelt and Harry Truman, who were great listeners. Eisenhower's press conferences as President were a disaster.

John Kennedy was a reader, who put together a brainy group of writers to assist him. Unfortunately, Lyndon Johnson kept most of Kennedy's staff and strategy in place when he became President. Johnson destroyed his presidency by not understanding that although he was a terrific listener, he was a poor reader who hardly understood anything he read.

Drucker says, "Few listeners can be made, or can make themselves, into competent readers—and vice versa. The listener who tries to be a reader will, therefore, suffer the fate of Lyndon Johnson, whereas the reader who tries to be a listener will suffer the fate of Dwight Eisenhower. They will not perform or achieve."

There are probably a half dozen ways to learn. Drucker offers some other examples. Winston Churchill learned by writing, and like many writers, did so poorly in school that he considered it pure torture. Beethoven was a writer and sketcher.

Others learn through discussion and hearing themselves talk. Drucker pointed out that successful trial lawyers and medical diagnosticians often fall in this latter category as did Drucker himself.

Some people are hands-on learners who absorb information by doing. Builders and mechanically oriented people often fall into this category. Active learning strategies like shop classes and labs are usually good for these students.

Some learn by mulling it over. Sara Blakely is the founder of Spanx and the world's first self-made female billionaire. Sara says that "thinking is actually a hobby" for her. She only lives a few blocks from her Buckhead area office, but every morning she gets on the Atlanta "Beltway" (Interstate 285) and drives around it...just so she can think.

Schools have historically been organized around the idea that there is only one way or one best way to learn.

Drucker says that it is really hard for students who learn differently.

Fortunately, thanks to Howard Gardner and others, schools are beginning to introduce "Differentiated Learning" strategies. But widespread implementation of these strategies may still be decades away.

If you or your child learns differently than the way an instructor teaches, you may have to develop your own differentiated learning strategy like Ben Carson did. To be fair, it's difficult for a teacher to accommodate 5 or 6 different learning styles in a classroom. The world class teachers pull this off but not every teacher will. Take responsibility for your education and for your child's education.

Jeff Sutherland, co-founder of the Scrum Project Management System offers the following true story in his new book titled *Scrum*:

Professor Stanley Eisenstat has been the instructor in the notoriously difficult, Computer Science 323 course at Yale University.

Former student turned tech entrepreneur, Joel Spolsky wanted to know if there was any correlation between time spent on class projects and the grade received. Spolsky discovered there was no correlation, but the results were more interesting than that.

He found the fastest "A" students outpaced the slower "A" students by an incredible 10:1 margin. In other words, they were 10x faster on class projects and got just as good of a grade. So what's the career application?

Rapid learning and work pace are strong indicators of innate talent. In a rapidly changing world, you will want to focus on careers where you can learn new material in the shortest time and where you can complete tasks quickly and efficiently.

Your learning style will be impacted by the aptitudes listed in the previous chapter on talent. If you are low in *Structural Visualization* or the ability to "See in 3D", you may struggle with science or geometry. Johnson O'Connor has years of research suggesting that students who score low in the aptitude they call *Graphoria*, may struggle with school work because much of it is tilted toward that aptitude.

It's wise to remember that many people we now regard as geniuses struggled in school. Albert Einstein did not speak until he was four and didn't read until he was seven. Both his teachers and parents thought he was developmentally slow. Later, he was expelled from one school and refused admittance to the Zurich Polytechnic School. Most would agree that he ended up doing well. Isaac Newton and Thomas Edison both did poorly in school.

What is your best way, or best combination of ways to learn? Are you a reader, listener, writer, talker, doer, or thinker?

More Thoughts on Learning Path

"Tell me and I forget. Teach me and I remember. Involve me and I learn."
~Benjamin Franklin, Inventor

"Everybody is a genius. But if you judge a fish by its ability to climb a tree, it will live its whole life believing that it is stupid."
~Albert Einstein, Scientist

"Lecture continues to be the most prevalent model in secondary and higher education but produces the lowest rate of retention."
~David Sousa, Author, *How the Brain Learns*

"It is the genius of the student that is the driving force behind all learning."
~Thomas Armstrong, Educator

"Anything that is worth teaching can be presented in many different ways. These multiple ways can make use of our multiple intelligences."
~Howard Gardner, Harvard University Professor

"...Forget about the math and concentrate on what your son can do well. Success is achieved by the development of strengths, not by the elimination of weaknesses. Name any successful person. Does this person have weaknesses? You bet!"
~Marilyn Vos Savant, Guinness Book High IQ Scorer (228)

CHAPTER 7

Your Skills Path

While the first five strength dimensions tend to have a natural, innate or genetic basis, the next two strengths are primarily developed. The next dimension of your *STRENGTHSPATH* is your **SKILLS**. These are your developed ability, mastery, proficiency, competency, know-how and how-to, including methods, steps, order, sequences, strategies, tactics, tool use and technology use. A skill is an ability developed through deliberate systematic effort, intentional practice and often supported by role models, mentoring, training and coaching. **Skills are what you add to talents in order to transform them into deliverable strengths**.

While talents are innate and enduring, skills are developed over time. In his book, *What's Your Genius?*, Jay Niblick talks about what he calls "The Simple Mistake". Jay describes a major problem in our culture when he writes, "The vast majority of people assume there is no real difference between talents and skills. They fail to appreciate just how fixed the neural networks that control these talents really are."

Corporate selection expert Jim Barrett frames this discussion by talking about the difference between aptitude and ability. Barrett writes, "Aptitude should not be confused with abilities. Present skills and capabilities are not aptitudes. Aptitudes are about potential, which is not necessarily realized at the present time."

Jim and Jay are correct. Innate, inborn, natural talent is the underlying foundation of successful performance. But they are different from skills, which must be developed or learned. That doesn't mean skills aren't important. They are a critical component of your strengths mosaic. I don't know about you, but I don't want a "naturally talented" doctor who hasn't gone to medical school or had lengthy internship, ad-libbing through my abdomen.

One reason for the confusion between talent and skill is they often are used interchangeably. We can say that someone is a skilled musician and we can also say that same person is a talented musician. But they really refer to two very different pieces to the puzzle. Again, talent you are born with and skills are something you develop and add to the talent in order to turn it into a strength.

Another reason for the confusion is that there are those in our culture who still believe natural talent doesn't exist. There are those who believe that with enough practice and hard work, anyone can do anything. But the science and the evidence just will not support that.

Math requires some knowledge, which we will cover shortly. But much of mathematics is a skill. Basic arithmetic skills are adding, subtracting, multiplying and dividing. Computing ratios, rates and percentages is basically skill oriented, although it does require some knowledge.

The practical application of fractions, percentages, ratios and proportions, logarithms, slide rule, practical algebra, geometric constructions, and essentials of trigonometry are mostly skills with a bit of foundational knowledge. Making change is mostly a skill. Performing operations with units such as cups, pints and quarts is also mostly a skill.

The relative ease with which you learn and then use these skills is your numerical aptitude, which I often call numeracy.

General Skills

Mathematics – Using numbers to communicate, evaluate and solve problems

Reading – Understanding letters, words and sentences

Speaking – Conveying information effectively by talking

Writing – Conveying information effectively through words and sentences using penmanship or keyboarding

Listening – Giving attention, asking questions and discerning important points

Learning - Recognizing, relating, assimilating and applying new information

Driving – Operating a motor vehicle

Computing – Operating a computer

Skill Types and Levels

Working skills might be thought of as job specific applications and levels of general skills. Take driving for example. For many jobs, it's just a matter of getting back and forth from work. For an outside salesperson, driving might be ¾ of their job. For a UPS driver operating a larger vehicle, more skill might be required. Driving an 18-wheel tractor-trailer rig, a bit more. A professional NASCAR or Formula One driver would require a whole different kind of skill at a whole new level. And the underlying natural talents required would be completely different for each level.

Similarly, operating a computer is now a job skill that is increasingly necessary for most jobs. In today's world, basic computer skills, keyboarding and familiarity with software like those found in the Microsoft Office Suite are becoming as critical as learning to drive. For one job it might be operating point-of-sale software in a retail environment or doing some simple word processing. Another job might include equipment maintenance, software installation and hooking up a few peripherals like a printer. Another level would be trouble-shooting and repair, then networking, programming and technology design.

Specialized Skill Set

Most jobs require some form of specialized skill set. Surgery is a specialized set of skills and so is accounting. So are waitressing, selling, teaching and any other job you can think of. The precise skill set required will be different from position to position, company to company and country to country. The skill set will also change over time at an increasingly rapid pace. This means that learning is becoming a critically important general skill.

More Thoughts on Skill

"What I do have are a very particular set of skills; skills I have acquired over a very long career."
~ Bryan played by Liam Neeson, from the movie *Taken*

"Have enough sense to know, ahead of time, when your skills will not extend to wallpapering."
~Marilyn Vos Savant, World's Highest Recorded IQ

"Everyone has a chance to learn, improve, and build up their skills."
~Tom Peters, Author and Speaker

"Mastering music is more than learning technical skills. Practicing is about quality, not quantity. Some days I practice for hours; other days it will be just a few minutes."
~Yo-Yo Ma, Musician

"Have you ever played a video game that didn't have escalating levels of difficulty? Well, life can feel like play, too, when we purposefully engage in activities that demand we test and develop our skills."
~Brandon Burchard, Author and Speaker

CHAPTER 8

Your Knowledge Path

The next step on your STRENGTHSPATH is **KNOWLEDGE**. It often builds synergy with skill as it works on top of the talent/passion foundation. Where skill is about mastering methods, steps and sequences; knowledge is about terminology, principles, policies, rules, information, concepts, theories and facts. In a strengths context, knowledge can be described as an organized body of information, often of a factual nature and sometimes of a procedural nature. It would be information that would make performing a certain type of work possible.

As an example of pure knowledge, I keep three resources in my library. One is a construction dictionary. It has 648 pages of construction oriented terminology. It doesn't show me how to build a thing. That would move into skills, a separate but related strengths dimension. It would help me communicate with tradesmen more accurately.

The second is a copy of the *Uniform Building Code*. This is a set of building rules and regulations designed to keep us all safe in the event of an earthquake or other catastrophe.

Again, this resource is very knowledge oriented and doesn't move into building skills.

I also own a pocket dictionary of art terms. It doesn't help me paint or draw or sculpt. It would help me communicate with artists.

In his terrific book, *Now, Discover Your Strengths*, Marcus Buckingham explains, "You need factual knowledge, which is content. For example, when you start to learn a language, factual knowledge is the vocabulary. In the same vein, salespeople must spend time learning their product features. Pilots must learn call signal protocols. Nurses must know exactly how much Novocain is appropriate for each procedure. No matter what your skills or talents you won't excel at painting if you don't know that red and green paint, when combined, create the color brown. Factual knowledge such as this gets you in the game. The second kind of knowledge is experiential, which isn't taught in classrooms or found in manuals. Rather it is something you must discipline yourself to pick up along the way and retain."

Knowledge can also be divided up into general knowledge, working knowledge and detailed knowledge.

General Knowledge

General knowledge includes the types of information found in a source document, or knowledge of the general types of information covered in a specific subject field. General knowledge will allow you to use a source to find specific information when it is needed. For example, a general knowledge of *STRENGTHSPATH* strengths would help you know where to look for more knowledge of a certain type. A general knowledge of baseball might refer to a basic understanding of the rules, their purposes, the general subjects the rules cover and where to reference the rules.

Working Knowledge

Working knowledge includes general knowledge, plus knowledge of, and ability to recall important and commonly used information from the source. For example, a general working knowledge of strengths, would include the knowledge mentioned above, and also the ability to recall major commonly held ideas from the strengths movement and specific strengths practitioners. A working knowledge of baseball might include the tendencies of a particular player, team or manager and their strategy in a particular situation.

Detailed Knowledge

Detailed knowledge is thorough knowledge of all information contained in a source or set of sources. Using the strengths example again, a strengths coach or strengths practitioner would be expected to have detailed knowledge of a variety of strategies and methods to help a client, student or group discover, develop, describe and deliver their strengths in the workplace without having to look them up. This would include strategies and methods that are not frequently used. A detailed knowledge of baseball would allow you to manage, coach or otherwise oversee practices and games.

Some things you can learn from a textbook, a class, an online program, a parent or a friend. You can acquire knowledge through study and reflection. Some types of knowledge require experience. There are some things you just can't get out of a book. There are some things you can learn but you really can't be taught. Most of our education system is designed to impart knowledge, often in the form of rote memorization with very little explanation of how it relates to real life.

To excel or become world class in any given field, you will need to develop expertise. In other words you will need to become extremely knowledgeable in the area you want to work.

Terminology (Descriptions)

Every profession has a unique language that includes vocabulary, terminology, names for parts and pieces, names for equipment and tools. Medical billers and coders have to learn medical terminology.

Location

If you are a doctor, you will need to learn where each body part is located. If you are a lawyer, you may need to learn how the law library is organized and where to look for case decisions and legal precedents. If you are an information technology specialist, you need to learn where the computer components are located and how they fit together.

Understanding

Every profession involves pattern recognition, rules, principles, symptoms, and meaning along with cause and effect relationships. Knowledge allows you to create "distinctions". When I look inside a computer I say, "Yep, it's a computer." Hopefully, when my repair person at the Genius Bar looks, he or she knows with great precision exactly what each piece is and what it does. Distinction leads to accurate diagnostics. These aren't developed skills so much as they are about building an essential knowledge base.

Professional football players spend an incredible amount of time watching game film. This is not to build their skill. They are expanding their knowledge. When they watch film of themselves they are expanding self-awareness. They also watch film of the teams they will be playing to learn patterns and tendencies.

Whatever work you choose, you will need to develop awareness and understanding of systems, procedures, equipment, theories, rules, laws, codes, precedents and more.

The Knowledge To Get More Knowledge

In a world of accelerated knowledge and rapid change, life-long learning becomes a high priority. Learning how to learn is paramount!

Knowledge and Truth

Many, including some in the scientific field confuse knowledge and truth. The truth never really changes. 2 + 2 = 4. It will always equal 4. That is truth. Knowledge advances, expands and even changes. Prior to this writing, 2 elements have been added to the Periodic Table. I grew up with the knowledge that Pluto is one of 9 planets in our solar system. Scientists are now suggesting otherwise. Pluto has been demoted to "Dwarf Planet" status. But not so fast. The controversy continues.

More Thoughts on Knowledge

"A fork in the road for most careers is what we choose to do when we confront a vocabulary (from finance, technology, psychology, literature...) that we don't understand. We can either demand that people dumb down their discourse (and fall behind) or we can learn the words. It's hard to be a doctor or an engineer or key grip if you don't know what the words mean, because learning the words is the same thing as learning the concepts."
~Seth Godin, Author and Marketing Expert

"Research is creating new knowledge."
~Neal Armstrong, Astronaut

"Knowledge has to be improved, challenged, and increased constantly, or it vanishes...Today knowledge has power. It controls access to opportunity and advancement."
~Peter Drucker, Management Consultant

"Those people who develop the ability to continuously acquire new and better forms of knowledge that they can apply to their work and to their lives will be the movers and shakers in our society for the indefinite future."
~Brian Tracy, Author and Speaker

"To acquire knowledge, one must study; but to acquire wisdom, one must observe."
~Marilyn vos Savant, World's Highest I.Q.

"There is no substitute for accurate knowledge. Know yourself, know your business, know your men."
~Lee Iacocca, Former Chrysler C.E.O.

"Experts have their knowledge in order. When your knowledge is not in order, the more confused you become by definition."
~Nido Qubein, Author and Speaker

CHAPTER 9

Your Character Path

CHARACTER wasn't included in my earliest outlines of the book. It wasn't because I didn't think character was important. I thought it was critical. But I thought it was critical to happiness. I thought it was critical to a good marriage. I thought it was critical to friendship.

I just didn't see that much of a connection to high performance at work. Oh sure, I understood the importance of honesty for salespeople. But isn't that a given? Then I thought some more...and some more. Examples started coming to mind about careers ruined and performances undermined. And these were not necessarily creepy people. Many were figures I loved and respected from a distance.

There was the popular female vocalist with a powerhouse voice. She was the best in the world.

There was the world-class golfer at the top of his game. He made watching this sport fun again. He seemed destined to break every record on the books.

There was more than one arguably brilliant U.S. President, from both political parties. One was forced to resign and the other was impeached by the House of Representatives.

There were the U.S. House of Representatives members that continued to allow themselves insider information privileges on the stock market.

There were the leaders of a large energy enterprise who misrepresented financials, eventually bringing down the entire company putting thousands out of work.

There was the pastor, the parish priest and the football coach.

There were the brilliant Wall Street bankers whose decisions nearly brought down the United States economy, if not the world economy, causing millions to lose jobs.

There were two car companies that falsified gas mileage records leading their customers to believe they were buying a car that got better gas mileage than it really did.

And there is you and me. Haven't we all stumbled? Haven't we all had a lapse of character?

After reflecting on all that, I knew I had to write this section. For some readers it might be the most important. It might prevent a career-ending move.

When I write about character strengths, I mean moral qualities and decisions. In fact, character strengths are the ones we all can choose.

Consider the following:

Committed – Attendance, Punctuality, Follow Up
Hard Work – Industry, Diligence, Active, Busy, Initiative
Attitudes – Grateful, Humble, Humor, Cheerful, Fun, Mercy
Respectful – Authority, Honor, Polite, Kind, Fair

Attentive – Fully Present, Anticipation, Awareness
Courageous – Bold, Brave, Grit
Truthful – Sincere, Scrupulous, Trustworthy, Ethical
Excellent – Workmanship, Quality, Presentable, Hygiene
Restrained – Self Control, Discipline, Clean-Sober, Frugal
Safety – Security, Protection

Why is character so important? Great successes always require collaboration. Collaboration requires trust. And trust only flourishes where character qualities are pervasive.

Your character is a huge part of your reputation, what you are known for, and what today is often described as your personal brand.

Character and moral qualities are a crucial part of your *SUCCESSPATH* package, and they are all a matter of choice!

More Thoughts on Character

"Real character is doing the right thing, knowing that nobody's going to know if you did it or not."
~Oprah Winfrey, Television Personality

"I have a dream that my four little children will one day live in a nation where they will not be judged by the color of their skin, but by the content of their character."
~Martin Luther King, Jr., Civil Rights Leader

"Winning takes talent. To repeat takes character."
~John Wooden, Former UCLA Basketball Coach

"As you go to work, your top responsibility should be to build trust."
~Robert Eckert, Former C.E.O of Mattel Toys

"Ask yourself...mercilessly: Do I exude trust? **E-X-U-D-E**. Big word. Do I smack of trust? Think about it. Carefully."
~Tom Peters, Business Author and Speaker

CHAPTER 10

Your Other Strength Dimensions

Are there other pathways of strength? I believe there are. I plan to focus on a few of them in future books for specific audiences. But you may need to be thinking about them and integrating them now. At the beginning of this book, I shared, "A strength is any resource, internal or external, that can be turned into a marketplace contribution". Here is a list with short explanations to get you started:

Geography - Location/Culture Strengths

Certainly your location is a critical and often overlooked component of your STRENGTHSPATH. I was at a strengths workshop recently where speaker/author Steve Witt talked about this. He thinks it's one of the most important of the strengths dimensions that you can choose.

It fits within my definition of a strength... "Any resource, internal or external that can be used to make a marketplace contribution". Your location can have a lot to do with your ability to contribute.

In my job search workshops, I call this the **Nashville Principle**. If you want to work in the country music business you probably need to move to Nashville, Tennessee. This is true with many career choices. If you want to be an actor in film or television, Los Angeles is your place. If stage is your goal, New York is your place. 3D artists should consider Los Angeles, Vancouver or London. There are many more tech opportunities in cities like Seattle and Austin, or areas like Silicon Valley.

I know this has grown controversial, but I'm still a believer in American exceptionalism. We have many sins as a country that we need to make right. But this is still a land of opportunity where people from all over the world can come and make a successful life. You have the freedom to travel or relocate to a region that will best support the growth of your other strengths.

If you'd like to research further on this topic, you might check out *The Geography of Genius* by Eric Weiner.

Environment

Some people thrive when they work outdoors. They were made for it. I'm not. I did it for years working in the family construction business and couldn't wait to get inside. This also has to do with your internal temperature needs. It may seem trivial but I've witnessed a lot of workplace conflict over the thermostat.

Other strength issues may come in to play as well. Some people can't concentrate with co-workers close by. Their distraction filter is set differently. Others thrive in a group environment. There is a huge number of articles and online chatter around the Open Office Strategy embraced by Google and others. Some are calling it a failure while others are defending it. Different people thrive in different environments. Some tasks and activities are now being described as "Deep Work" and they may require a different atmosphere. You may want to consider altering your environment depending on the task at hand. Some of this may have to do with the introvert-extrovert personality dimension briefly described in the chapter on Personality.

Chronotype

Chronotype, also called a biological clock, refers to the behavioral demonstration of underlying circadian rhythms. An individual's chronotype is the biological tendency to sleep at a particular time during a 24-hour cycle. There are "clock genes" that influence metabolism, hormones, body temperature, cognitive function and sleep needs.

Sleep scientists often use lay terminology, larks for morning people and owls for night people. This can be a big deal for some individuals. I've had friends and family members who operate toward the extremes. Don't think this is something they can control.

I worked for 16 years in an organization that had two different categories of sales people. One classification went to work at 8 or 9am. The other went to work at 2 or 3pm. Chronotype was an important strength to consider when selecting one position or the other.

Your Chronotype will drive your unique Window Of Optimal Performance or your "WOOP" time. Most of us have a 6 to 8 hour window each day where we are most effective. Ideally this should match up with your job.

Climate and Seasons

Looking back at my report cards, I always got better grades in the first and fourth quarters of the school year. This was consistent throughout school. I believe I suffer a bit from S.A.D. or Seasonal Affective Disorder and that may have impacted my performance.

My wife suffers terribly in the heat. I hate the cold. Both of our dispositions are affected by temperature. We've moved to a climate that generally works for both of us.

Pace

Are you the tortoise, the hare or something in between? Are you a sprinter, marathoner or middle distance runner? I often use a metronome as a prop in my workshops because it is such a good illustration of our internal pace. Some of this may be driven by your percentage of fast twitch and slow twitch muscle, which is based on genetics. It is something like torture for a fast-paced person to work in a slow-paced environment or a slow-paced person to work in a fast-paced environment.

The Bible talks about being "Unequally Yoked". It's referring to spiritual values but the concept surely applies to your pace. You generally will want to partner with people who match your velocity.

Spiritual Gifts

I plan to write another book where this subset of strengths plays a more prominent role. I was raised in the church and I've seen these strengths operate powerfully in faith communities. If you are curious about this topic or would like a head start, let me recommend a few resources.

They can be found in the *Recommended Reading* section at the back of this book.

Experience

What type of experience did you get in your last job or first job? Most job search candidates undervalue their early work experiences. Many play down experience in fast food, retail or jobs that demand physical labor. You were exposed to a lot more than you think.

Imagine two job search candidates with identical experience. Each walks into an interview having worked two years at the same McDonalds.

The first candidate is asked about their experience and responds:

"I just flipped burgers, that was pretty much it".

Then the second candidate walks in with identical experience but responds:

"My first job was at McDonalds. It was the greatest experience of my life. I still have friends that I made while working there. I'm no-where near the person I was when I started. I'm grateful for everything they taught me.

I learned how to:

Work with the public
Be responsible
Show up on time
Work under adverse conditions
Handle irate customers

Solve problems and put out fires
Make customers feel comfortable
Work as a team member
Be accountable and work under authority
Implement repeatable systems
Increase my efficiency
Organize, plan and set up
Display ordinary items in an extraordinary way
Process payments
Up-Sell...Do you want fries with that?

The **training was amazing**... It was **great**... It was **wonderful**... I would **do it all over again**..."

The second candidate painted a picture of what they experienced and **how they grew**.

Same experience... who gets the job?

You can learn to understand the strengths in your experiences, and give quality responses!

School

In his crazy-wonderful book, *Secrets of a Buccaneer-Scholar,* James Marcus Bach talks about *Schoolism* – the belief that schooling is the necessary and exclusive way to get a good education. Bach describes "Education" as the "you" that emerges from the learning you do.

Clearly, education can happen in or out of school. That being said, School, including diplomas, report cards, grade point average, degrees, certificates or certifications can be a strength. Even a record of some coursework can be a positive.

Bandwidth

In his book *The Acorn Principle*, Jim Cathcart talks about bandwidth as the capacity to acquire or add capacity. It is the amount of information we can process at one time. This is something akin to RAM inside a computer or a dial up vs. broadband internet access. If you're not up- to- speed with computer technology, think about the difference between the garden hose you use in the yard and the hose used by the local fire department.

I believe most of our bandwidth is directly related to our synaptic connections, resulting aptitude profile and learning style set up. In other words, we may have tremendous ability to add capacity in one area, yet be limited in another.

Thinking Style

Cathcart also talks about three different styles of thinking: Operational, Strategic and Conceptual. He reports that 80% of the population are Operational Thinkers. They prefer to focus on one thing at a time and deal with each item separately. About 18% are Strategic Thinkers. They process several ideas at once and consider the relative value of each alternative. Conceptuals, who see the big picture and the relationships between everything, compose 2% of the population.

Tools

Certainly tools are external resources that can be turned into marketplace contributions. At a basic level, this might include appropriate work clothes and transportation to and from work. It might include a work truck with very specific tools, a laptop computer or a computer repair kit. In my case, it includes my MacBook Pro and my Career Development Library. Whatever work you do, I recommend building a great set of tools.

Tribe

Your tribe is the people you hang out with. It is an external resource that can be leveraged into a marketplace contribution. In *The 6 Reasons You'll Get the Job,* Debra Angel MacDougall and Elisabeth Harney Sanders-Park contend that the right associates will land you a job or promotion and the wrong associates will hold you back. Many organizations are looking at your online friends. They are asking, "Do the people you know add value to our organization, or could they be a cause for concern?" Some companies are looking at a candidates *Klout* score before they hire for certain positions.

Adversities

Defeats, disappointments, set backs, difficulties, problems and challenges can build wisdom and resilience. Legendary investor Warren Buffett reportedly won't invest in a company where the owner/leader hasn't experienced multiple failures.

Disabilities

Many of the so-called disabilities or limitations are constraints that can be a source of focus. Like the Da Vinci's *Vitruvian Man* ideal, the hypothetical *Vitruvian Brain* ideal is in rapid decline. A disproportionate number of high level corporate CEO's and entrepreneurs have learning disabilities including dyslexia. It could be argued this so-called "disability" provided them with some advantage. Consider this list of achievers widely believed to be dyslexic:

Charles Schwab - Founder, Discount Brokerage Business
Craig McCaw - Cellular Phone Pioneer
John Reed - Led Citibank to the top of the industry
Scott Adams - Dilbert Creator
James Carville - Political Consultant
Cher - Singer, Entertainer
Charles "Pete" Conrad Jr. - Astronaut
Erin Brockovich - Activist
Whoopi Goldberg - Actress, Talk Show Host
Dr. Edward Hallowell - Psychiatrist
Bill Hewett - Co-founder, HP
Jay Leno - Host of the Tonight Show
Nelson Rockefeller - Former Governor of New York
Nolan Ryan - Hall of Fame Baseball Pitcher
Steven Spielberg - Film Maker
Thomas J. Watson Jr. - Former CEO, IBM
Henry Winkler - Actor

CHAPTER 11

STRENGTHSPATH Integration

Pulling Your Strengths Together

The marketplace rewards an integrated blend of passion, talent, skill and knowledge. One of the goals of this book is to better explain that integration. To better understand how talent, skill and knowledge enhance each other, consider the following examples:

Music is a passion
Rhythm is talent
Playing drums and dancing are both skills
Musical notation is knowledge

Baseball and Basketball are both passions
Eye-hand coordination is talent
Hitting a baseball and shooting a basketball are both skills
Studying the other team's pitcher or zone defense is acquiring knowledge

Numbers are a passion
Number memory and analytical reasoning are talents
Mathematics and using spreadsheets are skills
Accounting principles and tax law are knowledge

Art is a passion
Spatial vision is talent
Drawing or painting is skill
Art history is knowledge

In his book *Gifted Hands*, brain surgeon Ben Carson talks about this idea of strengths integration. He suggests that surgeons require an "Aptitude Talent" for "Structural Visualization" or being able to see in 3D. But to perform successful brain surgery, you must also acquire a set of skills that come through rigorous training, practice and experience. You need to acquire a very specific kind of knowledge including surgical tools and medical terminology. And you need a detailed understanding of neurological anatomy. None of this skill and knowledge building is probably going to happen without a lot of passion.

Increasingly, the marketplace is becoming very values conscious as leaders realize individual values are the chief components of organizational culture.

An understanding of learning style is more important than ever. Jobs are becoming obsolete everyday. In many cases, a job you are hired for today, won't even exist in a few years. Re-learning new roles quickly, including the new skills and knowledge that comes with them, becomes paramount.

Character is critical. Employers are frustrated. So many new employees hired don't understand the importance of regular work attendance and consistently showing up on time.

Dynamic Tensions

Dr. Timothy Butler is the Director of Career Development Programs at Harvard Business School. In his book, *Getting Unstuck: A Guide to Discovering Your Next Career Path,* he talks about this idea of "Dynamic Tensions".

As Butler explains it, "One part of the self finds attraction in one direction and another part of the self is drawn to an apparently contradictory direction." Butler believes that some people even become aware of this through images or spontaneous visions. One example might be the sensation of "walking a tightrope". Sometimes these images come up when listening to a popular song that somehow describes or explains the tension or contradiction you're experiencing.

In Chapter 2, *Your Passion Path,* I talked about Ed Catmull who had this pull to art, represented by his hero Walt Disney. But he also had this pull toward science, represented by his other hero Albert Einstein. He eventually resolved this conflict by pulling them together in computer animation, a new science based art form which he helped create.

In my workshops, I often give the example of my wife Susy who has two very strong competing values. One part of her is a regimented rule keeper and another part is an independent renegade. She resolved this with two jobs. During the week, rule keeping Susy worked with struggling kids in a continuation high school. Independent Susy was a Rock Star performer in a band every weekend.

Timothy Butler offered up a dynamic tension he calls, "Serving Others" vs. "Being The Star". The example he gave was Dr. Martin Luther King. As Butler explains, part of Dr. King's role, included both his willingness to serve and eventually sacrifice his life. It also included being in the spotlight and becoming something of a star.

In her book, *Mindworks*, trainer Anne Linden explains what Neuro-Linguistic Programing (NLP) practitioners call "Parts". Linden says, "By 'parts' I mean aspects or qualities of a person: the efficient part, the stay-at-home part, the nurturing part, the shopper part, the baby, the glamour girl and all the other selves, parts and facets that make up the whole individual, whether or not the person is conscious of them."

Learning to integrate these parts is the artistic side of career development. Like the snowflake, you are a completely unique, one-of-a-kind individual. This is why off-the-rack jobs always need some tailoring, just like a well-made suit of clothes.

Learning to integrate your parts, especially those in tension will require wisdom and some trial and error. It's a little like the story of the wizard and the magic carpet:

A younger wizard wanted a magic carpet just like the old wizard. The old wizard agreed to help and show the young wizard how to weave his own. When the magic carpet was complete, the young wizard was disappointed because it was very plain. The old wizard explained, "The more experiences you have, the wiser you become, the richer and more beautiful your carpet becomes".

Integrating all our parts, including the passions, talents, skills, knowledge and values with their inevitable tensions is like that.

Another relevant story in Chapter 2 was under the heading, *Finding Your Mash Up.* The story about the high school kid who stood up in the career direction assembly to explain that he liked walking and he liked turtles. Within minutes the Roadtrip Nation staff had him on the phone talking with a "Turtle Walker".

It really is possible to honor all your parts and dynamic tensions. How you can do that may require some time and creativity to pull it all together. You were created to do something absolutely unique and the clues sit before you.

More Thoughts on Integration

"A winner is someone who recognizes his God-given talents, works his tail off to develop them into skills, and uses these skills to accomplish his goals."
~Larry Bird, Former Professional Basketball Player

"We suggest that you take a close look at knowledge, skills, and talents. Learn to distinguish each from the others. Identify your dominant talents and then in a focused way acquire the knowledge and skills to turn them into real strengths."
-Marcus Buckingham, Author and Speaker

"Talent x Investment = Strength"
~Tom Rath, Author and Speaker

"Your talents, passions and conscience together add up to a whole person...If your job requires your skills but not your talents, you will never tap into the genuine and instinctive part of yourself."
~Stephen R. Covey and Jennifer Colosimo, Authors

"When you surround yourself with hugely talented, passionate, dedicated, and genuinely kind people you will succeed in whatever you do."
~Kip Tindell, Founder of The Container Store

CHAPTER 12

Sprint To A Strengths Based Future

One purpose of this book is to give you a basic introduction or overview to eight strength components. I hope I've done that in the previous chapters of this book.

Now I'd like to move into the primary purpose. I'd like to offer some basic steps to get you started on your unique *STRENGTHSPATH*. Each of these steps will be covered in more detail with the following chapters. But let's get you started.

I'm going to give you **Five Job Shaping Projects**. I will be loosely using concepts from the **Agile Platforms**. These project management frameworks originated at Toyota, and are now being implemented by thousands of individuals, teams and organizations in all types of industries all over the world. Building contractors use Agile as do farmers. Agile has diversified into multiple frameworks including *Lean*, *Extreme Programing*, *Kanban*, and *Scrum*. You can transform your career using the same project management framework that the world's top companies are using to build products.

There are several benefits of the Agile framework. It's very simple to start using but when the need is there, it can expand into a very sophisticated set of tools. If you are already using one of the Agile platforms in a work context, this will build on something you already understand. If you're not familiar with Agile, this provides a brief introduction that may benefit you later.

Using the Agile terminology, I break each of my career development and job search coaching projects into segments known as a **"Sprint"**.

A **"Sprint"** is a time-boxed process of one month or less, where an individual or team implements a goal-oriented backlog of tasks on a list. This list goes on a "Do" - "Doing" - "Done" Board sometimes going by the Japanese name "Kanban". I like the "Do" – "Doing" – "Done" format because it perfectly matches the **Y.E.S.** time frames I talked about in the chapter on passion. Is there a **Yearning** before you begin the items on the "Do" list? Is there **Engagement** with a growing sense of energy and timelessness while you're "Doing" the items? Is there a sense of **Satisfaction** after you've "Done" the items on the list? The Kanban Board can provide a terrific strengths check-in.

You can easily build your own on a sheet of paper, poster board, grease board or using an online tool. If you go with the online option, I recommend Trello.com which is what I use. It's easy to learn and can be reconfigured and shared easily.

Do	Doing	Done

When coaching, my strengths oriented career development sessions include:

Sprint Planning – Preview the "To-Do List Backlog"
Daily Scrum (15 Min) – Yesterday/Today Review Update
Sprint Reviews (1 Hr) – Demo Learning-Action-Results
Sprint Retrospectives (1 Hr) – Discussion of Process

The Job Shaping Sprint Series includes:

Sprint One: **Discovering Your Strengths**
Sprint Two: **Describing Your Strengths**
Sprint Three: **Directing Your Strengths**
Sprint Four: **Developing Your Strengths**
Sprint Five: **Delivering Your Strengths**
Sprint Six: **Dealing with Weakness**
Sprint Seven: **Detours and Roadblocks**

When I work with clients on Job Search, the Sprint Series includes:

Sprint One: **Strengths Discovery**
Sprint Two: **Targeting Companies and Positions**
Sprint Three: **Resume and Marketing Materials**

Sprint Four: **Interview Preparation**
Sprint Five: **Direct Contact and Hidden Jobs**
Sprint Six: **Employer Postings**
Sprint Seven: **Relationship Networking**
Sprint Eight: **Staffing and Search Firms**
Sprint Nine: **Search Challenges**

I offer an expanded version of each Sprint when working with clients. But let's look at condensed versions of the Job Shaping Sprints you can do on your own, with a partner, team or another coach.

CHAPTER 13

Your Discovery Sprint

The contemporary poet Shawn Carter aka Jay-Z says it well, "Every human being has a genius level talent. There are no chosen ones. You have to find what you're great at and tap into it."

Your *STRENGTHSPATH* is in part discovered. As you've seen, you have a completely unique set of success aptitudes and abilities that are innate and natural. You were born with them. Most of us wander around completely oblivious to these innate *strengths*. Yet, they can be clearly identified through a discovery process using a number of proven tools.

I've poured through hundreds of resources over the last 10 years looking at the different ways those active in career development help their employees, students or clients discover their strengths. There are seven approaches that have a good track record. I recommend triangulating. Get three witnesses. Use several of these methods for the most accurate results.

The ***Achievement List Analysis*** method is very useful. I have often used a version of this in my workshops with what I call the *Factory Settings* exercise. I have class members list all the activities and subjects they either enjoyed or were good at, starting with their earliest memories. We then look for patterns of success, including activities, aptitudes and approaches that suggest certain strengths. Bernard Haldane pioneered the SIMS, *System to Identify Motivated Strengths* and the *Dependable Strengths Articulation Process*. Arthur Miller developed SIMA, *System for Identifying Motivated Abilities*. Richard Bolles wrote the best-selling career selection book of all time titled, *What Color Is Your Parachute?* Each of these programs are built around identifying personal success or achievement stories, then carefully reviewing each for patterns of passionate interest and natural talent. One potential downside is that some struggle with writing. For those an interview process can be substituted.

The **Activity List Analysis** is another effective strategy and works primarily with current tasks. Grab a sheet of paper and draw two lines creating room for 3 categories. The first category is for *Awesome Activities* that make you feel strong. The second category is for *Average Activities* that leave you feeling neutral. The third is *Awful Activities* that leave you drained. Every time you do an activity, place it in a category. Marcus Buckingham recommends a version of this with his *Love It – Loathe It* exercise.

Peter Drucker used a method he borrowed from both the Jesuit and Calvinist faith communities. I call it **Anticipation Analysis**. Set a goal, anticipate the outcome and review the process for clues about your strengths. Drucker followed the process for 50 years, using it to identify the tasks he should take on and those he should leave for others.

Appraisal Analysis is another method that can point you in the right direction. Any form of feedback including report cards, performance reviews, compliments and requests to do work can all offer clues. Sometimes it can be helpful to ask those who know you best, "Hey, what do you see in me? What am I good at?"

Consider doing what I call an *Appearance Analysis*. What keeps showing up at your front door? The ancient documents we sometimes refer to as the Old and New Testaments were written by over 40 authors over a 1500 year period. Many of these writings are what we might refer to as "Call and Response" narratives. At the end of the day, I believe in a Creator-God who has placed each of us on the planet with a specific purpose in mind. If you take those ancient documents seriously, as I do, you might consider the variety of ways He communicated those purposes including reoccurring dreams and orchestration of events.

My research suggests the Chinese were using vocational *Assessments* 4,000 years ago. In the last 100 years, career counselors have used a variety of assessments to help with career discovery. I believe work sample assessments are the most accurate, but psychometric assessments, using trait choice, or more recently, situational judgment methods can be useful self awareness tools. When debriefing an assessment report with a client, I always ask them to re-write any section they feel doesn't accurately describe them. **I use assessments because of the answers they suggest, but also because of the questions they raise.** Without assessments, those seeking to discover their STRENGTHSPATH must pull primarily from personal experience and an occasional burst of imagination.

Frank Parsons wrote *Choosing A Vocation*, published in 1909 and oversaw the Vocational Bureau at the Boston Y.M.C.A.. He seems to have favored simply **Asking Questions** or using a structured set of inquiries. In his brilliant little book, *How To Find The Work You Love,* Laurence G. Boldt talks about this new paradigm of vocational guidance. He writes:

"While traditional vocational guidance depends upon a testing process to identify your interests and/or skills, **the new paradigm uses a series of carefully crafted questions designed to help you tap into your creative passion**. While it appears simple, this latter technique requires individual commitment, responsibility, and self-awareness. Because the goal of this process is not simply a job that is a good fit but a work you truly love and can devote your life to, more will be required of you. You can take a test to discover a number of careers you may be suited for, but no test will ever tell you what you love to do - that you will have to discover for yourself. Yet, if you make the effort to persevere until you have found the work you truly love, you will be rewarded with a lifetime of adventure, meaning, and joy." Boldt's books may have the most creative and useful sequence of career selection questions ever assembled.

I believe in the genius of all these methods and use each of them with my clients. Assessments in my view don't replace carefully crafted questions or success story analysis. But neither do carefully crafted questions and success story analysis fully replace assessments. They are bookends to a thorough and integrated discovery process.

Exercises

1. **Inquiries –** Write out answers to the following questions or have a partner ask and take good notes. You could also record the answers or the conversation and transcribe it later.

Imagine? Imagine waking up tomorrow morning, and everything about your job is changing. Your work is shifting to something amazing. What exactly are you seeing, hearing and feeling? Most importantly, what are you doing? How are you doing it? Where are you doing it? Who are you collaborating with? How do you recognize that this is in fact your dream job?

Contribution Inquiries

Impact? What strengths show up when you walk in the room? What are your contributions? Where do you add value? Where do positive results show up as a result of your activities?

Indispensible? What is the role or roles where you have been indispensible? Where are you the Linchpin?

Invitations? What tasks are you invited to perform? When do people ask you back? What are your "Encore Activities" where people want a repeat performance?

Passion Inquiries

iDreams? What are your dreams?

I'd Rather Be…? What's your "I'd rather be" bumper sticker?

Intense Interests? Which sections of the bookstore/ magazine section pull you? Where do you spend money after the bills are paid? What are your regular online stops?

Idle? What do you do with your free time? What do you do after work and on weekends?

Ignition? What gets you going? What activities give you energy?

Illumination? What are your "Lights On" subjects? Which topics of discussion light you up?

Incubation? What are your day dreams? What are you always thinking about? What's stewing in your mental crock pot?

iPod? What music do you listen to? What are your top 10 favorite songs of all time? Why do you like them? What are your favorite lyrics?

iCalendar? What's on your calendar? What do you schedule?

IMAX? What are your favorite movies or TV shows?

Talent Inquiries

Inborn Inclination? Identify your *"Factory Settings"*. What did you love doing at ages 5, 6, 7, 8, 9, 10, 11, 12, 13, 14? What were you good at?

Instincts? What activities and tasks do you have an instinctive feel for? What's your version of a "green thumb"?

Individualized Moments? Someone has said we all have about 20,000 moments a day. What are your "Made-For-This-Moments"? What are the times or activities where you felt like you were made to do that?

Impossibility? What do you find *impossible* not to get involved with? What can't you <u>not</u> do?

Insanely Great? What are you insanely great at?

Innovative? Where or when are you the most creative? What are the situations where you come up with ideas?

Improvisational? When do you easily go off script?

Insight? What do you see or notice that other people don't?

Improve/Increase? In what areas or activities do you grow the fastest? What are the subjects you learned quickly and easily? What are the skills you picked up without much effort?

Ingenious/Intelligence? What is your genius? How are you smart?

Idle? Which of your talents aren't getting used?

iAptitudes? List the following intelligences in order as you think they show up in your personal hierarchy. Word Smart? Picture Smart? Body Smart? Logic/Math Smart? People Smart? Self Smart? Nature Smart? Existential Smart? Music Smart?

iActivities? What's inside you trying to get out? What activities must you do?

iApproach? Are you better at Execution, Influence, Relationship Building or Strategic Thinking? List them in order.

Personality Inquiries

Identity? How would you describe yourself?

Ideogram? What symbol or symbols would you use to describe yourself? !?@#$&<>/=+-

Intrapersonal or Interpersonal? Do you ponder or socialize? Are you intra-active or interactive?

Intuitive? Sensing? Do you prefer to use your intuition or senses?

Improvise? Plan? Do you like structure or making it up as you go?

Independent? Interdependent? Do you prefer to go solo or with a partner?

Idiosyncrasies? What are your quirks?

Values Inquiries

Ideals? An ideal world/work/workplace would have more...?

Important? What's important to you in a job?

Ideology? How would you describe your philosophy?

Injustice? What are the wrongs in the world that must be set right? What makes you angry?

Iconoclast? What traditional belief would you most like to challenge?

Intolerable? What is difficult for you to tolerate?

Irritations? What day-to-day irritations do you experience?

Learning Style Inquiries

Instruction? How do you learn? Listen? Read? Doing? Writing? Talking? Drawing? Thinking?

Skill Inquiries

If? If your life depended on naming a skill at which you're in the top 1% of the world, what would it be?

Increase? What skill would you enjoy increasing 25% in the next year?

Incomplete? Where are you still trying to grow and get better?

Inadequate? Where do you need to grow?

Improvement? If there was one thing you'd start doing differently tomorrow to unleash more of your potential, what would it be?

Instructor? What have you learned how to do? If you had to train or coach someone, what would it be?

Instrument? What is your "Alchemical Object", something like a wand that allows you to work magic? For Harold, in the children's book by Crockett Johnson, it was his Purple Crayon. For Picasso, it was a paint brush. For Jimi Hendrix, it was his guitar that he reportedly slept with. For Dr. Ben Carson, it was a scalpel. For Stephen Curry, it's a basketball behind the 3-Point line.

Knowledge Inquiries

Information Jump? What kind of information just seems to jump in your head?

Informed? What subjects are you an expert in?

Instructors? Who are your current teachers, trainers or coaches?

Instruction? If you had to teach a subject, what would it be?

Idiolect? Where is your vocabulary strongest?

Ignorance? What is your biggest area of ignorance?

Insatiable? What subjects are you most curious about?

Character Inquiries

Integrity? Where are you the best at keeping your commitments?

Infidelity? When do you not keep your commitments?

Ignored? What internal direction or calling have you ignored?

Impulsive? What do you do without thinking?

Misc Inquiries

Internal Clock? What's your chronotype?

Immortality? Imagine you extended your life 10 years or could do a set of activities for eternity. What is your vision of paradise on earth? What about that vision really captivates you?

Imitation/Idols? Who are your role models or heroes? Who would you like to be more like? Are these role models symbolic or do you actually want to do what they do each day?

Iceberg? What's the best thing about you that very few people know?

2. **Awesome-Average-Awful** – Get a sheet of paper and use two lines to create three sections. In the first section, write down activities that make you feel awesome. In the second section average. In the third section, write what makes you feel awful. Look for patterns of strength.

3. **Assessments** – I suggest a D.I.S.C. inventory, Marcus Buckingham's StandOut and Myers-Briggs inventory from www.type-coach.com. I highly recommend Strengthsfinder 2.0.

4. Create Your Nine Panel Strengths Summary

In the back of the book, you will find a nine panel model with a box for each of the strength dimensions I've shared. Included are Passion, Talent, Personality, Values, Learning Style, Skills, Knowledge, Character and Collection for miscellaneous other Strengths. You may wish to recreate it in a larger size and fill-in what you've learned about yourself in each box.

CHAPTER 14

Your Description Sprint

Business author Tom Peters said, "You had better have a clear mark of distinction brilliantly communicated." Management Consultant Peter Drucker said, "Most Americans do not know what their strengths are. When you ask them, they look at you with a blank stare..."

The Description Sprint allows you to begin putting your strengths in a language to **describe, demonstrate and display** what you do best on a Resume, a Portfolio, an Online Profile or in a Job Interview. This Sprint should also help you at your performance review or a team meeting where assignments are divided up. We all need to establish and publish an "I'm Great At This" list that helps us communicate with partners, colleagues and hiring managers what we do best.

1. Write/Share a S.T.A.R. Story Paragraph

S.T.A.R. stands for Strength, Target, Action, Result.
Write a short Success Story about yourself from work, school, sports, a hobby or volunteer activity. Briefly, with

a sentence for each of the four points, list a Strength you used, the Target you defined, the Action you took and the Result you achieved.

2. Elevator/Party/Network Description

You should be able to give a clear concise description of your work in 30 seconds. This is often called an "Elevator Pitch" but it is useful outside the elevator.

3. Interview Talking Points

Prepare talking points for the 5 interview questions below. Have a partner ask you the questions, as if you were in a job interview. Don't spend any longer than 30 seconds on each answer.

Tell me about yourself...?
What are your strengths?
What is your superpower?
What is your kryptonite/biggest weakness?
The Facebook Interview Question
"On your very best day at work, the day you come home and think you have the very best job in the world, what did you do that day?"

4. Take the Fascination Advantage Assessment

Sally Hogshead has developed a wonderful assessment specifically designed to help you describe your strengths.

Go to http://www.howtofascinate.com and complete the assessment. Read your report and consider ways to use the descriptions in the materials we have prepared.

5. Update Your Resume and LinkedIn Profile

Both your resume and your LinkedIn Profile should brilliantly communicate your strengths. The resume should be very targeted toward a specific job description.

CHAPTER 15

Your Direction Sprint

Direction, especially career direction, should be well informed by a solid understanding of your natural and developed *strengths*. You should set clearly defined goals based on who you are. Make sure you climb the right mountain and make sure your career ladder is leaning against the right wall. Most people have trouble setting up the right targets. They struggle with setting and reaching goals. Getting clear on goals and reaching them becomes much easier when these targets are oriented around your unique strengths.

In this Sprint you will be turning your Talents into Targets.

1. Describe Your Dream Job

Using your strengths as a foundation and your Ideal Day/ Week/Month as a clarifier, write a paragraph or a page describing your dream job. Focus on the tasks that are passion and talent based. Make most of your description about what you want to do on a daily basis.

2.   Create A Contribution Statement

Write your contribution statement beginning with the word "Because". Follow it with a summary of the problem you will solve or solution you will provide.

Contribution Statement Example:
Because less than 20% of workers use their strengths everyday, I will train and coach individuals how to discover, develop and deliver their unique strengths in the marketplace.

3.   Create a Professional Objective Statement

Include:
- Role and responsibilities
- Functional tasks you will perform
- Ultimate direction and progression

4.   Create a Target Market Statement

Include:
- Geographic flexibility
- Industries you want to pursue
- Preferred size, style and culture of an organization

5.   Create a Target Company List

If there are limited opportunities to pursue your dream job in the company where you work, you will need to look outside. Google Maps is an excellent way to develop your Target List. Go to **https://maps.google.com** and type in the type of organization that hires people to do what you want to do.

CHAPTER 16

Your Development Sprint

In order to fully realize potential, your natural success abilities must be grown, expanded, refined, polished, advanced and nurtured. Recent findings on the plasticity of the brain suggest that we can do this throughout life, even into old age.

In this Sprint you will be developing your natural passion and talent into full-blown strengths.

1. Identify Your Role Models

List several role models here. Who are the experts already working at your Dream Job?

2. Become an Expert by Reading/Listening

Author Bob Philips once told me, "You can become an expert by reading 10 books on a subject". Put yourself on a reading/listening program depending on your learning style. Many books are available in recorded version. Develop a library of materials from the best people in your field. Find **Podcasts** and **Ted Talks** that relate your interests and industry.

3. Informational Interviews

Inspirational speaker Charlie "Tremendous" Jones used to say, "You'll be the same tomorrow except for the books you read and the people you meet". Talk with people already doing what you want to do. Conduct informational interviews with people already working in fields you are interested in. This can be done by phone or more ideally in person. Make sure that some of them are world class at what they do.

4. Introductory Classes

Sign up for a class at the University, Community College, Adult School or Online options including Khan Academy, Lynda, Coursera, Udemy and Udacity. Find a workshop or seminar.

5. Join Your Tribe

Find your people. Go to **MeetUp.com** and see if there are meetings related to your field. If not, start one. Join groups dedicated to your field. Attend a convention. Join **LinkedIn** Groups and start connecting with people who are already doing what you're doing.

6. Practice - Get Your 10,000 Hours

If you want to become the "Best-Version-Of-Yourself", you will need to practice!

CHAPTER 17

Your Delivery Sprint

Action, performance and contribution is the endgame of *The STRENGTHSPATH Principle*. A lot of people take strengths assessments, throw them in a drawer and never see them again. Seth Godin describes a similar phenomena with what he calls "Transformational Tourism":

"I bought the diet book, but ate my usual foods."
"I filled the prescription, but didn't take the meds."
"I took the course... well, I watched the videos... but I didn't do the exercises in writing."
"Merely looking at something almost never causes change. Tourism is fun, but rarely transformative."

And Timothy Butler warns, "Recognizing the deeper patterns of the self is not enough. We must find the will to act, even in very small ways, so that our new imagination becomes more and more what we live everyday."

Delivering your strengths, by executing your unique approaches, using your aptitudes and implementing activities that make you feel strong, are the critical steps to realizing your full potential.

APPROACH

The first way to deliver your strengths and optimize your work is by adjusting your "Approach". In chapter 3, I shared the example of comedians and the different ways they approach their craft.

There are a lot of ways to be successful at the same job. In my work as a manager, I watched sales people reach the pinnacle of success with quite different strengths and ways of going about their day to day work. This is possible with most jobs, including the job of running the country. Let's consider the first four American presidents. Did they all have similar strengths that led to similar ways of operating in office? Not at all.

George Washington was the military strategist who projected an image of consistency and stability while serving as a great unifier. He had no great gift as a visionary but his cool even temperament served us well as he united a young country.

The second president, **John Adams,** was a phenomenal orator and skilled debater. It was said that he could hold Congress in rapt attention for hours as he waxed on eloquently about his positions on Britain, France and so on. He was at his best when voicing his opposition to a real or perceived foe.

Thomas Jefferson was completely different than either. Unlike the orator Adams, Jefferson hated public speaking. In fact, he hated it so much that he refused to give the traditional State of the Union message to Congress each year. He was a grand strategist that loved sitting at his desk, thinking and writing. He wrote out the State of the Union speech and had his assistant read it.

James Madison was different still. He was a very precise thinker and the consummate networker. He loved roaming the floors of Congress, meeting one on one, collaborating and building alliances to accomplish his goals for the country.

All four could rightly be held up as examples of great presidents. But each understood their strengths and weaknesses and proceeded to shape the job around who they were. List any other four great presidents in history and you'll see much of the same principle at work. **Lincoln**, the melancholy who suffered great bouts of depression, worked quite different than the energetic **Theodore Roosevelt**. **Jimmy Carter** is arguably the most effective ex-president in history and has had great impact working on a number of important problems around the world. While in office, he worked long days. His successor, **Ronald Reagan** worked much shorter days, was a famous napper and joked, "I know hard work never killed anybody, but why take the risk".

I have similar stories outlining vastly different approaches taken by the nine U.S. Supreme Court Justices and the four key generals who led America's efforts in World War II. They had the same job but each took a totally unique approach based on their strengths.

Helping you identify and then implement your unique approach is where a strengths assessment is the most valuable. If you have taken both Marcus Buckingham's StandOut 2.0 Assessment and Gallup's Strengthsfinder 2.0, this is a good time to begin integrating the report. Both are designed to help you dial-in your unique approach to work.

Find an experienced strengths oriented career development coach to help you implement the results.

APTITUDE

The second way to deliver your strengths and optimize your work is by using your "Aptitudes". A good understanding of your aptitudes will help you better understand why you struggle with some activities and easily succeed with others. You will want to eliminate activities from your job description when they are built on low aptitudes and add activities when they are built on high aptitudes.

An understanding of your aptitudes will also help you shift your approach. In some cases, certain aptitudes may be so fundamental to a job you will need to make a change. Understanding your aptitudes will help you make that change.

ACTIVITIES

The third way to optimize your job and deliver your strengths is to shift the "Activities" or tasks. Here are a few exercises to help.

1.   Ideal Day/Week/Month

Write down your ideal day. It should be a day where you do exciting activities that contribute and add value.

2.   Build a SUCCESSPATH Start List

From your Discovery Sprint in chapter 13, transfer ideas of activities that make you feel strong. That will make up your "START" List.

3. Implement the "STRENGTHSPATH MATH" Addition Strategy

ADD one activity into your weekly routine from the "START" list. These are the activities that make you feel strong.

The key to any or all of these strategies is remembering that added value must remain your focus. The idea is to spend the maximum amount of time working on activities that allow you to increase your performance and make bigger contributions.

CHAPTER 18

Your Dealing with Weakness Sprint

Sara Blakely, Founder of Spanx and the first woman to become a self-made billionaire says, "As soon as I could afford to hire my weaknesses I did". An important part of maximizing your strengths is learning to minimize, marginalize and manage your weaknesses.

Peter Drucker wrote, "We all have a vast number of areas in which we have no talent or skill and little chance of becoming even mediocre. In those areas, a person, and especially a knowledge worker should not take on work, jobs, and assignments. One should waste as little effort as possible on improving areas of low competence. It takes far more energy and work to improve from incompetence to mediocrity than it takes to improve from first rate performance to excellence. And yet most people, especially most teachers and most organizations concentrate on making incompetent performers into mediocre ones. Energy and resources and time should go instead into making a competent performance person into a star performer."

For many of us, the effort expended on turning a weakness into a strength is the single biggest roadblock to our success. Even if you are good at many things, there is a hierarchy of strengths, and that means you have relative weaknesses.

ACTIVITIES

The first way to deal with your weakness is similar to the last chapter on delivering your strengths. You need to begin removing the tasks you don't like and are not good at. Here are a few exercises to help.

Weakness Inquiries

Incompetence? What are you incompetent at?
What is your Kryptonite?
Where is your shoe nailed to the floor?
Where is your boat tied to the dock?

1.   Daily/Weekly/Monthly Weaknesses

Write down the daily, weekly and monthly tasks or activities that drain you, sap your energy and keep you from spending more time on your strengths.

2.   Build a SUCCESSPATH Stop List

Put together your "Kryptonite" list on a separate sheet with activities that make you feel weak. This list will include activities you want to "STOP" or at least reduce.

3. Implement the "STRENGTHSPATH MATH" Subtraction Strategy

SUBTRACT one activity out of your weekly routine from the "STOP" list. In some cases, you can do this, and no one will notice or care. In other situations, you will need to negotiate with a supervisor or colleague. Here are some ideas to help with your task "Subtraction" strategies:

- **Pop It** - Like letting air out of a balloon, reduce the amount of time spent on the task.
- **Slop It** - You can be sloppy with some things and some things have to be done perfectly. Learn the difference and adjust.
- **Swap It** - If you can't stop an activity, see if you can trade activities with someone who loves the task.
- **Shop It** - If you can't swap it, then shop it. See if you can outsource it to a professional.
- **Chop It** - If that is not a practical option, see if you can divide it up into increments so it's not as intolerable.
- **Prop It** - Use props or tools to make the task easier. Add music. Reward yourself with a cookie.
- **Workshop It** - Go to a workshop or seminar and learn to get better, maybe even how to enjoy the task.
- **Op It** - There are some projects you shouldn't take on because they don't fit your strengths or the strengths of the organization. There are "bad sales". Opt out!

Like adding strengths to your schedule, the key to any or all of these strategies is remembering that added value must remain your focus. Again, the idea is to spend the maximum amount of time working on activities that allow you to increase your performance and make bigger contributions.

CHAPTER 19

Your Daily STRENGTHSPATH

At the end of the day, the *STRENGTHSPATH* Principle is all about how you spend your days. No one has invented the shiny toy that makes up for the loss you feel when day after day you end up doing what you don't enjoy.

Over the years I have collected dozens of examples of how successful people from a variety of professions spend their days. Here are five "day" samples. Some are very detailed. Each gives a feel for how that person regularly spends their time.

David Brenner, Comedian

"I have a routine I follow every day. About 3 o'clock I'll sit down with a stack of that day's newspapers and weekly magazines, and I'll go though it and clip stuff out that I think is interesting. And then I'll go on the internet and print out anything that might work from the fields of science or medicine or health. Initially, I might have no idea what I'm going to say about it; I just know that there's something there that could be funny. And then I'll watch CNN or another news channel and see what's happening there. And I make up these cards that have the story line on them. And then I go on stage and hold up the card and hope something funny happens from it."

Michael Bloomberg, Financier, Mayor of New York

"I still think a perfect day is one where I'm hopelessly overscheduled. Jog early in the morning and get to work by 7:00 AM; a series of rushed meetings; phone call after phone call; fifty more voice messages and the same number of e-mails demanding a reply; a hurried business lunch between a myriad of stand-up conferences to solve personnel, financial, policy problems; perhaps give an interview to some foreign newspaper where we needed publicity; often make an image building speech at some local conference in person or by satellite video conferencing to the other side of the world; constantly welcome visiting clients; an early dinner with customers or a group of employees, followed by a second one with friends (where I actually get a chance to stop talking and eat); fall into bed, exhausted but satisfied with the day's accomplishments. That's the best weekday one could ever have!"

Maya Angelou, Poet, Novelist

"When I'm writing, everything shuts down. I get up about five, take a shower, and don't use the Rose Geranium bath gel from Floris – I don't want that sensual gratification. I get in my car and drive off to a hotel room. I can't write in my house. I take a hotel room and ask them to take everything off the walls so there's me, the Bible, Roget's Thesaurus, and some good, dry sherry, and I'm at work by 6:30. I write on the bed lying down – one elbow is darker than the other, really black from leaning on it – and I write in longhand on yellow pads. Once I'm into it all disbelief is suspended, it's beautiful. I hate to go, but I've set for myself 12:30 as the time to leave, because after that it's an indulgence, it becomes stuff I'm going to edit out anyway.

Then back home, shower, fresh clothes, and I go shopping for nice food and pretend to be sane. After dinner I re-read what I've written… If April is the cruelest month, then eight o'clock at night is the cruelest hour, because that's when I start to edit and all that pretty stuff I've written gets axed out. So I've written 10 or 12 pages in six hours, it'll end up as three or four if I'm lucky.

But writing is really my life. Thinking about it when I'm not doing it is terribly painful, but when I'm doing it… it's a lot like if I was a long-distance swimmer and had to jump into a pool covered with ice: It sounds terrible, but once in it and two or three laps done, I'm home and free."

Warren Buffet, Investor

"Well, first of all, I tap-dance into work. And then I sit down and read. Then I talk on the phone for seven or eight hours. And then I take more home to read. Then I talk on the phone in the evening. We read a lot. We have a general sense of what we're after. We're looking for seven footers. That's about all there is to it… I am doing what I would like most to be doing in the world, and I have since I was 20. I choose to work with every single person I work with. That ends up being the most important factor. I don't interact with people I don't like or admire."

Dale Cobb

Donald Trump, Real Estate Developer

"I don't do it for the money. I've got enough, much more than I'll ever need. I do it to do it. Deals are my art form. Other people paint beautifully on canvas or write wonderful poetry. I like making deals, preferably big deals. That's how I get my kicks.

Most people are surprised by the way I work. I play it very loose. I don't carry a briefcase. I try not to schedule too many meetings. I leave my door open. You can't be too imaginative or entrepreneurial if you've got too much structure. I prefer to come to work each day and just see what develops.

There is no typical week in my life. I wake up most mornings very early, around six, and spend the first hour or so reading the morning newspapers. I usually arrive at my office by nine, and I get on the phone. There's rarely a day with fewer than fifty calls, and often it runs to over a hundred. In between I have at least a dozen meetings. The majority occur on the spur of the moment, and a few of them last longer than fifteen minutes. I rarely stop for lunch. I leave my office by six-thirty, but I frequently make calls from home until midnight, and all weekend long.

It never stops, and I wouldn't have it any other way. I try to learn from the past, but I plan for the future by focusing exclusively on the present. That's where the fun is. And if it can't be fun, what's the point?"

If you'd like a well-researched resource that summarizes the schedules of 161 historical figures, I recommend Mason Currey's *Daily Rituals*. His single page accounts chronicling the daily agendas of people like Albert Einstein, Mozart,

Buckminster Fuller, Toni Morrison, Benjamin Franklin, Ann Rice, Nicola Tesla, Frank Lloyd Wright and dozens of others is truly fascinating. Like all high achievers, they were aligned with their strengths and it showed up in how they designed their days.

How does possessing a certain set of strengths impact how an individual approaches each day? In short, if your schedule is aligned with your strengths, you will greet the day with desire. To the extent your schedule is misaligned, you will greet the day with dread. The most important thing you can do is make sure that your daily agenda is driven by your design.

Success Movement strategists from Ben Franklin to Tony Robbins have recommended starting and ending each day with a set of questions. Here is the set I recommend based on the principles in this book:

The 7 STRENGTHSPATH Morning Questions:

What am I passionate about today?
How will I use my natural talents?
How will today reflect my personality?
How will I live out my values?
How will I use my learning path to add skill or knowledge?
How will I live from conscience and character?
How will I contribute?

The 7 STRENGTHSPATH Evening Questions:

How did I live with passion today?
How did I use my natural talents?
How did I reflect my personality?

How did I live out my values?
How did I use my learning path to add skill or knowledge?
How did I live from conscience and character?
How did I contribute?

Add these questions to your Sprint work explained in chapters 12 through 17.

CHAPTER 20

The Extended Life Path

Swiss-American psychiatrist Elizabeth Kubler-Ross is arguably one of the most knowledgeable people of all time on the process of death and dying. She is a legend in the Hospice movement and is maybe the most famous for her helpful 5-stage grief model.

In *Death Is of Vital Importance* she writes, "It is very important that you only do what you love to do. You may be very poor, you may go hungry, you may lose your car, you may have to move into a shabby place to live. But you will totally live. And at the end of your days, you will bless your life because you have done what you came here to do. Otherwise, you will live as a prostitute. You will do things only for a reason to please other people and you will not have lived. And you will not have a pleasant death. If, on the other hand, you listen to your own inner voice, to your own inner wisdom, which is far greater than anyone else's as far as you are concerned, you will not go wrong, and you will know what to do with your life. Then time is no longer relevant."

In this chapter, I'm going to invite you to do a couple of thought experiments with me. The first one is a small stretch. The second, for some may be a bigger stretch, but I invite you to hang with me.

The first thought experiment is adapted from Dan Sullivan's *Pure Genius* Workshop and is based on his *Strategic Coach* Principles. In the workshop, he walks the participants through a "**Life Extension**" exercise similar to the one below.

First, select the age you believe you are most likely to die. Most people select something around current life expectancy numbers and add or subtract a few years based on family history.

Now, think about your lifestyle choices. Could they be improved? How about your diet? How about your exercise habits? With better choices, how many years do you think you could extend your life? Most people agree they could extend their life 10 years or more with improved lifestyle choices.

What would you love to do with those extra 10 years? What activities would you love to be doing? What talents would you be using? What causes would you be involved with?

Could you begin working with those activities, talents and causes now? Even if you're overwhelmed, could you do it for 10 minutes a day?

This is the second thought experiment I'd like you to consider. It requires a little bit of set up.

I come from a place of Faith, but my observation is that the Christian Church has not always been an accurate steward of the ideas and concepts found in Scripture. And most of us haven't really taken the time to read the Bible or check the facts on our own. Of course we haven't done that with Science books either but that's another story for another time.

If you want to consider any of this on a deeper level, I recommend a book on the afterlife by Randy Alcorn. It's called *Heaven*, but don't let that fool you. It blows up many of the myths about what the Jewish-Christian Scriptures really teach about the life after this one. Alcorn contends that the church has been complicit in characterizing eternity as an unending church service more like Gary Larson's *Far Side*. In one of his cartoons, a man with angel wings and a halo sits on a cloud doing nothing with no one nearby. He has the expression of someone marooned on a desert island with nothing to do. The caption reads, "I wish I'd brought a magazine".

Alcorn notes, "We do not desire to eat gravel. Why? Because God did not design us to eat gravel. Trying to develop an appetite for a disembodied existence in a non-physical Heaven is like trying to develop an appetite for gravel." Alcorn walks us through the Scriptures highlighting the verses that point us to a very different idea of Heaven including, "A resurrected life, in a resurrected body, with a resurrected Christ on a resurrected Earth".

Towards the end of the book, Alcorn asks the question,

"Will Our Life's Work Continue?"

Alcorn builds a good case that it will. So here is the last part of my thought experiment....

If you were to select a career that would carry into the afterlife, what would it be?

What is your vision of "Paradise on Earth"?

What is the part that really captivates you?

Could you begin working with those activities, talents and causes now? Even if you're overwhelmed, could you do it for 10 minutes a day?

As a very imperfect follower of Jesus Christ, the thoughts in this book have additional personal meaning. As a natural cynic and Snopes devotee, I believe in a personal God who created the universe. How He did it, I have no idea. Maybe it was in six twenty-four hour time frames, or maybe He used a longer process akin to what we would call evolution. I see the honest study of Scripture and the honest study of Science as very compatible, even desirable, possibly necessary.

I believe the evidence is overwhelming that Jesus died for my sins and miraculously rose from the dead. Based on that alone, I am expecting an amazing life beyond this one that is without end. I also believe that Jesus taught there is a life God rewards and part of that is connected to how we develop and deliver the different components of our unique strength. Jesus taught on Service, Contribution and Getting Results (Bearing Fruit). Jesus taught on the importance of using our Talents, directing our Passions, growing our Character, living by His Kingdom Values and He clearly called us to a life of Mission. The whole Bible can be viewed as a series of "Call and Response" narratives about a God who invites us to partner in stewarding the planet.

I believe Jesus will return. I love the chapter title in N.T. Wright's book, *Surprised by Scripture*. Wright says, "Jesus is Coming – Plant a Tree". I'm not a big fan of apocalyptic, dooms day, end times theology. Increasingly, I'm a fan of Harold Eberle, who suggests in his book, *Victorious Eschatology,* that the Kingdom of God is growing and it will continue to grow until it fills the Earth.

CHAPTER 21

The Greatest General

I often close my workshops with the following story that continues to motivate me in my work with clients around their natural talents and strengths:

A man died, went toward the light, and found his way to St. Peter at the Gates of Heaven. I guess we all have our own questions and curiosities at that moment and this individual was no different. He rushed up to St. Peter and blurted, "I've had this burning question all my life. I'm just dying to know the answer."

St. Peter said, "Yes... I can see that... We've been expecting you."

The man responded, "Actually, I've been a military history student my whole life, and I've just got to know, who was the greatest general of all time?"

Peter quickly replied, "Oh, that's an easy one... It's that guy right over there." (pointing across the garden)

The man scratched his head and thought a minute, a bit confused.

"But I knew that guy... he was a janitor at the office where I worked."

Peter replied, "You're absolutely right, but he would have been the greatest general of all time.... IF... he had become a general!"

And that story illustrates a truth that should haunt us all...

Most people go from cradle to office cubicle to casket, never using their greatest talents and potential strengths. It's a truth that disturbs me. I believe it should disturb us all.

But the good news is, it doesn't have to be this way. You've finished this book. Now you can get started on your own unique *STRENGTHSPATH*. You can begin **discovering** your natural talents. You can begin **developing** those talents into full-blown strengths. And you can begin **delivering** them in the workplace today!

If I can help you on your *STRENGHSPATH*, please contact me soon!

AFTERWORD

Whenever I coach a client, present a training program or sit down to write a book chapter, I am acutely aware that life is sometimes so much more complicated than the best advice I could offer. Any single piece of wisdom is always incomplete. Most groupings of wisdom are incomplete as well. This book is actually about 50% shorter than the one I originally wrote. I became convinced that many in my intended audience wouldn't read a longer book, at least initially. So you have the shortened version with some of the material left on the "cutting room floor".

I am also aware that most readers who start a book, don't finish it and fewer still actually implement even one of the ideas presented. Obviously that won't help.

The STRENGTHSPATH Principle is an integrated, interdependent set of strategies. My observation and experience is that they work together synergistically. A lot has been written recently, pushing back on authors who encourage us to find and follow their passion. One book, *Do What You Love, The Money Will Follow* by Marsha Sinetar is one example. The title, while catchy, is incomplete. Sinetar's advice is way more detailed than the title suggests. I doubt the critics of her book have seriously put the suggestions to any serious test. Based on the shallow criticism I see, most haven't even read the first two chapters.

If you want to try these strategies using an a la carte process you can. But like the critics, I think you'll be disappointed. Passion without talent, skill and knowledge doesn't get you very far. If you have those four components, but try to implement them in an organizational culture where you are misaligned, you will still beat your head against the wall. That's why I didn't write a book encouraging you to simply find and follow your passion. It's not because it doesn't work, it's just incomplete!

Because you can't do everything at once, the book is laid out in a strategic sequence. Work through the first 10 chapters to get a basic understanding of the different strength components. Then begin working through the Sprint chapters. You will run into roadblocks trying to merge onto your STRENGTHSPATH. You will hit potholes and come up to detours. But if you stay with it, I believe you'll find the onramp to your own personal 8 lane super highway.

~See You On The Path!!!

Dale Cobb

BIBLIOGRAPHY

Prologue

Chapter 1   The STRENGTHSPATH Principle

1. Brad Plumer, *"Only 27 Percent of College Grads Have a Job Related to their Major"*, *The Washington Post*, May 13, 2013, accessed May 3, 2016, https://www. washingtonpost.com/news/wonk/wp/2013/05/20/only-27-percent-of-college-grads-have-a-job-related-to-their-major/ .

2. Marcus Buckingham, *The Truth About You* (Nashville: Thomas Nelson, 2008), 7.

3. Nicholas Lore, *The Pathfinder* (New York: Fireside/ Simon and Schuster, 1998), 11-13.

4. Zig Ziglar, *See You At The Top* (Gretna, Louisiana: Pelican Publishing, 1977), 6.

5. Kip Tindell, *Uncontainable: How Passion, Commitment, and Conscious Capitalism Built a Business Where Everyone Thrives* (New York: Hachette Book Group, 2014), 53.

6. Jim Clifton, *The Coming Jobs War* (New York: Gallup Press, First Printing, 2011), 106.

Chapter 2   Your Passion Path

1. Mihaly Csikszentmihaly, *Flow: The Psychology of Optimal Performance* (New York: Harper Classics, 2008), 88.
2. Oprah Winfrey, *The Best of Oprah's What I Know For Sure* (New York: The Oprah Magazine, Hearst Corporation, 2000), 39.
3. Nathan Gebhard, Brian McAllister and Mike Marriner with Jay Sacher, Alyssa Frank, Annie Mais, Jaime Zehler and Willie Witte, *Roadmap* (San Francisco: Chronicle Books, San Francisco, 2015), 156-157.
4. Ed Catmull, *Creativity, Inc. – Overcoming The Unseen Forces That Stand In The Way Of True Inspiration* (New York: Random House, 2014), 8-20.
5. Janet Attwood Interview with Lilou Mace, Youtube, October 28, 2013, Accessed May 3, 2016, https://youtu.be/78NGfghtyTo .

Chapter 3   Your Talent Path

1. Lady Gaga and Jeppe Laursen, Song Lyrics: *Baby You Were Born This Way* (Santa Monica: Streamline Records, 2011).
2. Don O. Clifton and Paula Nelson, *Soar With Your Strengths* (New York: Dell Publishing, 1992).
3. Marcus Buckingham and Don O. Clifton, *Now, Discover Your Strengths* (New York: Free Press/Simon and Schuster, 2001).
4. Bob McDonald and Don E. Hutcheson, *Don't Waste Your Talent* (Marietta, Georgia: Longstreet Press, 2000), xi.

5. Scott Adams-Creator, "*The Knack*" from *Dilbert: The Complete Series* (DVD) (Culver City: Sony Pictures, 2000), Season 1-Episode 9.

6. Howard Gardner, *Multiple Intelligences* (New York: Basic Books, New York, 1993), 17-26.

7. Margaret E. Broadley, *Your Natural Gifts* (McLean, Virginia: EPM Publications, 1977), 3-7.

Chapter 4   Your Personality Path

1. Dr. Phil McGraw, *Life Strategies* (New York: Hyperion, 1999), 268.

2. Roger Birkman, *True Colors* (Nashville: Thomas Nelson, 1995).

3. Colin Powell, *It Worked For Me* (New York: Harper Collins, 2012), 95-96.

Chapter 5   Your Values Path

1. Nathan Gebhard, Brian McAllister and Mike Marriner with Jay Sacher, Alyssa Frank, Annie Mais, Jaime Zehler and Willie Witte, *Roadmap* (San Francisco: Chronicle Books, San Francisco, 2015), 171-172.

2. Eduard Spranger, *Types of Men: the Psychology and Ethics of Personality* (Halle, Germany: M. Niemeyer, 1928).

Chapter 6   Your Learning Path

1. Ben Carson with Gregg Lewis & Deborah Shaw Lewis, *You Have A Brain* (Grand Rapids: Zondervan, 2015), 90-93.

2.   *Gifted Hands* (DVD) (Culver City: Sony Pictures, 2009).

3.   Peter Drucker, *Managing Oneself* (Boston: Harvard Business Review, 2008), 11-19.

4.   Sara Blakely Interview with Darren Hardy (Plano, Texas: Success Magazine, January 2016), Track 2, CD Insert.

5.   Jeffrey D. Wammes, Melissa E. Meade, Myra A. Fernandes, *The Drawing Effect: Evidence for Reliable and Robust Memory Benefits in Free Recall*, The Quarterly Journal of Experimental Psychology, Volume 69, Issue 9, 2016, 1752-1776.

Chapter 7   Your Skills Path

1.   Jay Niblick, *What's Your Genius?* (St. James Books, 2009), 26.

2.   Jim Barrett & Kogan Page, *Ultimate Aptitude Tests* (London: Kogan-Page, 2012), 4.

Chapter 8   Your Knowledge Path

1.   Marcus Buckingham and Don O. Clifton, *Now, Discover Your Strengths* (New York: Free Press/Simon and Schuster, 2001).

Chapter 9   Your Character Path

1.   Stephen M.R. Covey with Rebecca Merrill, *The Speed of Trust* (New York: Free Press/Simon and Schuster, 2001).

2.   Jim Loehr, *The Only Way To Win: How Building Character Drives Higher Achievement and Greater Fulfillment in Business and Life* (New York: Hyperion, 2012).

Chapter 10   Your Other Strength Dimensions

1. Eric Weiner, *The Geography of Genius* (New York: Simon and Schuster, 2016).
2. James Marcus Bach, *Secrets of a Buccaneer-Scholar* (New York: Scribner/Simon and Schuster, 2009), 5.
3. Jim Cathcart, *The Acorn Principle* (New York: St. Martins Press, 1999).
4. Debra Angel MacDougall and Elisabeth Harney Sanders-Park, *The 6 Reasons You'll Get the Job* (New York: Prentice Hall Press, 2010).

Chapter 11   STRENGTHSPATH Integration

1. Timothy Butler, *Getting Unstuck: A Guide to Discovering Your Next Career Path* (Boston: Harvard Business Press, 2007), 57.
2. Anne Linden with Kathrin Perutz, *Mindworks* (Kansas City: Andrews McMeel, 1997), 205.
3. Amy Wrzesniewski and Jane Dutton, *Job Crafting Exercise* (Ann Arbor: University of Michigan's Ross School of Business, 2001).

Chapter 12   Sprint To A Strengths Based Future

1. Tycho Press, *Scrum Basics: A Very Quick Guide to Agile Project Management* (Berkley: Tycho Press, 2015).
2. Jeff Sutherland, *Scrum: The Art of Doing Twice the Work in Half the Time* (New York: Crown Business, 2014).
3. Tridibesh Satpathy-Lead Author, *Scrum Study: A Guide to the Scrum Body of Knowledge* (Phoenix: Scrumstudy, 2013).

Chapter 13   Your Discovery Sprint

1. Crockett Johnson, *Harold and the Purple Crayon* (New York: Harper Collins, 1955).
2. Laurence G. Boldt, *How To Find The Work You Love* (New York: Penguin Compass, 2004).
3. Insoo Kim Berg and Steven de Shazer, *The Miracle Question*, Developed in the 1970's for Brief Solution-Oriented Therapy.
4. Steve Dalton, *The 2 Hour Job Search* (New York: Random House, 2012).
5. Steve Roesler, *"What Can't You Not Do?"* Question (All Things Workplace Blog, Posted September 15, 2011, Accessed May 4, 2016), http://www.allthingsworkplace.com/2011/09/what-cant-you-not-do.html .

Chapter 14   Your Description Sprint

1. Peter Drucker, *Managing Oneself* (Boston: Harvard Business Review, 2008).
2. Stephen R. Covey and Jennifer Colosimo, *Great Work Great Career* (Bhopal, India: Franklin Covey India/ Manjul Publishing House, 2009).
3. Sally Hogshead, *Fascinate: Your 7 Triggers to Persuasion and Captivation* (New York: Harper Collins, 2010).

Chapter 15   Your Direction Sprint

1. Marcus Buckingham, *StandOut 2.0: Assess Your Strengths – Find Your Edge – Win At Work* (Boston: Harvard Business Review, 2015).
2. Tom Rath, *Strengthsfinder 2.0* (New York: Gallup Press, 2007).

Chapter 16   Your Development Sprint

1. Charlie "Tremendous" Jones, *Life is Tremendous* (Carol Stream, Illinois: Tyndale House, 1981).

Chapter 17   Your Delivery Sprint

1. Seth Godin, *Type Pad Blog Post* (April 28, 2016) http://sethgodin.typepad.com/seths_blog/2016/04/transformation-tourism.html
2. Timothy Butler, *Getting Unstuck: A Guide to Discovering Your Next Career Path* (Boston: Harvard Business Press, 2007), 155.
3. Marcus Buckingham, *StandOut 2.0: Assess Your Strengths – Find Your Edge – Win At Work* (Boston: Harvard Business Review, 2015).
4. Tom Rath, *Strengthsfinder 2.0* (New York: Gallup Press, 2007).

Chapter 18   Your Dealing with Weakness Sprint

1. Sara Blakely Interview with Darren Hardy (Plano, Texas: Success Magazine, January 2016), Track 2, CD Insert.
2. Peter Drucker, *Managing Your Career* (Boston: Harvard Business Review, 2007).

Chapter 19   Your Daily STRENGTHSPATH

1. David Brenner, *David Brenner's Day*, Comedian (America West Magazine, April 2001).
2. Michael Bloomberg, *Bloomberg by Bloomberg* (New York: John Wiley & Sons, 2001).

3. Maya Angelou, *Maya Angelou's Day* (Utne Reader, July-August 1998).
4. Siimon Reynolds, Compiler, *Thoughts of Chairman Buffett* (New York: Harper Collins, 1998).
5. Donald Trump with Tony Schwartz, *The Art Of The Deal* (New York: Ballantine Books, 1987).
6. Mason Currey, *Daily Rituals* (New York: Alfred A. Knopf, 2013).

Chapter 20   Your Extended Life Path

1. Elisabeth Kubler-Ross, Goran Grip, Ken Ross, *Death Is of Vital Importance: On Life, Death, and Life After* (Barrytown, New York: Station Hill Press, 1995).
2. Dan Sullivan, *Pure Genius CD Recording Set* (Chicago: Nightingale-Conant, 2003).
3. Randy Alcorn, *Heaven* (Carol Stream, Illinois: Tyndale House, 2004).
4. N.T. Wright, *Surprised by Scripture* (New York: Harper Collins, 2014).
5. Harold Eberle, *Victorious Eschatology* (Yakima, Washington: Worldcast Publishing, 2006).

Chapter 21   The Greatest General

1. Don O. Clifton and Paula Nelson, *Soar With Your Strengths* (New York: Dell Publishing, 1992).

Look for these coming titles in the SUCCESSPATH Series:

The STRENGTHSPATH Time Manager

The STRENGTHSPATH Guide to Selection and Hiring

*The SUCCESSPATH Strategies: A Guide
To Universal Success Principles*

*The STRENGTHSPATH Strategies:
Succeeding by Doing What You Do Best*

*Crazy Good: A STRENGTHSPATH Guide
to Discovering Your Natural Talents*

*Insanely Great: A STRENGTHSPATH Guide
to Developing Your Talents Into Strengths*

*Wildly Successful: A STRENGTHSPATH Guide
to Delivering Your Strengths in the Workplace*

The STRENGTHSPATH Manager & Leader

The STRENGTHSPATH Sales Person

The STRENGTHSPATH Parent

*Maximize Your Ministry: A STRENGTHSPATH
Guide to Doing What You Do Best*

The SUCCESSPATH Educator

The Daily STRENGTHSPATH

SUCCESSPATH Sprint Coaching

One-to-One Sprints ✷ 60-Minute Seminars ✷ Workshops

Modeling Projects ✷ Performance Research

Strengths Assessments ✷ Selection ✷ Outplacement

Strengths Oriented Career Development Sprints
Arrive! - Strengths Oriented Goal Sprints
Strengths Oriented Time Management Sprints
"A-Game" Sprints
Service Oriented Selling Sprints
Storyboarding – Customer Experience Journey Sprints

Connect Online

Follow Our SUCCESSPATH Sixty Second Seminars

LinkedIn https://www.linkedin.com/in/dalecobb

Facebook https://www.facebook.com/
successpathcareerdevelopment/

Twitter https://twitter.com/strengthspath

Website http://www.successpathcareerdevelopment.com

Vimeo https://vimeo.com/dalecobb

YouTube https://www.youtube.com/user/daleacobb

Tumblr https://www.tumblr.com/blog/dalecobb

Contact

Dale Cobb
P.O. Box 870
Grover Beach, CA 93483
805.668.9600

SUCCESS PATH

RECOMMENDED READING

First, I'm aware that successful career development is not everyone's obsession. This may be the only book on strengths based career development that you ever read. If this book peaked your interest, there is a lot more to know.

Your motivations will be unique. I'm in the process of writing other resources for specific audiences with unique interests. Until those books are released, I've offered up a sizeable list to keep you learning.

There are a large number of strengths based resources now available. One of my goals in writing this book was the removal of silos and integration of several *Strengths Movement Families*. For the most part, the strengths movement families don't acknowledge each other's existence. Some of this isolation is probably due to competition in the business arena. Some of it is probably due to honest differences on how an individual or team should go about discovering, developing and delivering strengths in the workplace. Whatever the reasons, I think the average strengths enthusiast and seeker of success is the loser in this.

The resources are loosely organized by families of thinking. In some cases, this is difficult because a few of the writers are more eclectic, embracing and integrating methods and ideas.

Drink deeply from many wells!

Gallup/Marcus Buckingham Family

Soar With Your Strengths, Don O. Clifton and Paula Nelson

Now, Discover Your Strengths, Marcus Buckingham and
Donald Clifton

Strengths Finder 2.0, Tom Rath

Stand Out 2.0, Marcus Buckingham

Go, Put Your Strength To Work, Marcus Buckingham

The Truth About You, Marcus Buckingham

Trombone Player Wanted DVD Series, Marcus Buckingham

Find Your Strongest Life, Marcus Buckingham

The One Thing You Need To Know, Marcus Buckingham

First Break All The Rules, Marcus Buckingham and Curt
Coffman

Strengths Based Leadership, Tom Rath and Barrie Conchie

*Follow This Path: How the World's Greatest Organizations
Drive Growth by Unleashing Human Potential*, Curt
Coffman and Gabriel Gonzalez-Molina, Ph.D.

*Human Sigma: Managing The Employee-Customer
Encounter*, John H. Fleming and Jim Asplund

Animals Inc., Kenneth A. Tucker

*Strengths Based Parenting - Developing Your Children's
Innate Talents*, Mary Reckmeyer and Jennifer Robinson

Strength Based Selling, Tony Rutigliano and Brian Brim

Discover Your Sales Strengths, Tony Rutigliano and Benson Smith

Teach With Your Strengths, Rosanne Liesveld, Jo Ann Miller with Jennifer Robison

Are You Fully Charged?, Tom Rath

Entrepreneurial Strengthsfinder, Jim Clifton and Sangeeta Bharadwaj Badal, Ph.D.

The Coming Jobs War, Jim Clifton

The Power of 2: How to Make the Most of Your Partnerships at Work and in Life, Rodd Wagner and Gale Muller

STRENGTHSQUEST: Discover and Develop Your Strengths In Academics, Career, and Beyond, Donald O. Clifton, Ph.D. and Edward "Chip" Anderson, Ph.D.

12 Elements of Great Managing, Rodd Wagner and James K. Harter, Ph.D.

Johnson O'Connor/The Highlands Family

Don't Waste Your Talent, Bob McDonald and Don E. Hutcheson

Hardwired: Taking the Road to Delphi and Uncovering Your Talents, Dr. Tom Tavantzis with Paul Jablow

Understanding Your Aptitudes, Johnson O'Connor Research Foundation

Your Natural Gifts, Margaret Broadley

Learning To Use Your Aptitudes, Dean Trembly

Know Your Real Abilities, Charles V. and Margaret E. Broadley

Structural Visualization, Johnson O'Connor

Ideaphoria, Johnson O'Connor

Unsolved Business Problems, Johnson O'Connor

Square Pegs In Square Holes, Margaret E. Broadley

The Unique Individual, Johnson O'Connor

Be Yourself: Analyzing Your Innate Aptitudes, Margaret E. Broadley

The Too Many Aptitude Woman, Johnson O'Connor

The Aptitude Handbook: A Guide to the AIMS Program, Aptitude Inventory Measurement Service

Rockport Institute Family

The Pathfinder - How to Choose or Change Your Career for a Lifetime of Satisfaction and Success, Nicholas Lore

Now What? The Young Person's Guide to Choosing the Perfect Career, Nicholas Lore and Anthony Spadafore

Job Search/Career Services Family

Job Search Magic, Susan Whitcomb

The Person Called You: Why You're Here, Why You Matter and What Should You Do With Your Life, Bill Hendricks

Why You Can't Be Anything You Want to Be, Arthur Miller Jr. with William Hendricks

Born For This: How To Find The Work You Were Meant To Do, Chris Guillebeau

Getting Unstuck: A Guide to Discovering Your Next Career Path, Timothy Butler

Choosing a Vocation, Frank Parsons, Ph.D.

Making Vocational Choices: A Theory of Careers, John L. Holland

Business Model You: The One-Page Method for Reinventing Your Career, Tim Clark, Alexander Osterwalder and Yves Pigneur

What Color Is Your Parachute?, Richard Bolles

How to Find Your Mission in Life, Richard Bolles

How To Find The Work You Love, Laurence Boldt

Zen And The Art Of Making A Living, Laurence Boldt

Career Satisfaction and Success, Bernard Haldane

How to Make a Habit of Success, Bernard Haldane

Young Adult Career Planning, Bernard Haldane

Job Power Now!, Bernard Haldane

6 Reasons You'll Get The Job, Debra Angel MacDougall and Elisabeth Harney Sanders-Park

Unlocking Your Sixth Suitcase, John Bradley and Jay Carty

Your Dream Career For Dummies, Carol L. McClelland, Ph.D.

RoadTrip Nation Family

Finding The Open Road - A Guide To Self-Construction Rather Than Mass Production, Nathan Gebhard, Brian McAllister and Mike Marriner

Roadtrip Nation - A Guide To Discovering Your Path In Life, Mike Marriner, Nathan Gebhard with Joanne Gordon

Roadmap - The Get-It-Together Guide for Figuring Out What To Do with Your Life, Nathan Gebhard, Brian McAllister and Mike Marriner with Jay Sacher, Alyssa Frank, Annie Mais, Jaime Zehler and Willie Witte

Franklin Covey

The 8th Habit, Stephen Covey
Great Work, Great Career, Stephen Covey and Jennifer Colosimo

U.K. Families

The Strengths Book, Alex Linley, Janet Willars and Robert Biswas-Diener
Average to A+, Alex Linley
The Strengths Way, Mike Pegg
The Strengths Toolbox, Mike Pegg

D.I.S.C – 4 Quadrant Personality Style Families

Self Awareness: The Hidden Driver of Success and Satisfaction, Travis Bradbury
The Platinum Rule: Discover The Four Basic Business Personalities and How They Can Lead You To Success, Tony Alessandra, Ph.D. and Michael J. O'Connor, Ph.D.
Leading From Your Strengths, John Trent and Rodney Cox
The Essential DISC Training Workbook, Jason Hedge
Who Do You Think You Are...Anyway, Robert A. Rohm, Ph.D. and E. Chris Carey
Positive Personality Profiles, Robert A. Rohm, Ph.D.
Personality Style at Work: The Secret to Working With Almost Anyone, Kate Ward
The 8 Dimensions of Leadership, Jeffrey Sugerman, Mark Scullard and Emma Wilhelm

Color Your Future, Dr. Taylor Hartman, Ph.D.

The People Code, Dr. Taylor Hartman, Ph.D.

True Colors, Roger Birkman, Ph.D.

Top Brain, Bottom Brain: Surprising Insights Into How You Think, Stephen M. Kosslyn, Ph.D. and G. Wayne Miller

Winning From Within: A Breakthrough Method For Leading, Living, and Lasting Change, Erica Ariel Fox

Social Style Management: Developing Productive Work Relationships, Robert Bolton and Dorothy Grover Bolton

The Four Elements of Success, Laurie Beth Jones

The Personality Compass: A New Way To Understand People, Diane Turner and Thelma Greco

Play Your Best Hand, Faith Ralston, Ph.D.

Personality Poker, Steven M. Shapiro

The Strategic Coach Family

Unique Ability, Catherine Nomura and Julia Waller with Shannon Waller

Unique Ability 2.0, Catherine Nomura and Julia Waller with Shannon Waller

Unique Ability 2.0 Discovery, Catherine Nomura and Julia Waller with Shannon Waller

Pure Genius CD Series, Dan Sullivan

The Kolbe Family

Powered by Instinct, Kathy Kolbe

The Conative Connection, Kathy Kolbe

Pure Instinct, Kathy Kolbe

Miscellaneous Families

What's Your Genius?, Jay Niblick

Where We Belong: Journeys That Show Us The Way, Hoda Kotb with Jane Lorenzini

Quiet: The Power of Introverts in a World That Can't Stop Talking, Susan Cain

Me, Myself, And Us: The Science of Personality and the Art of Well-Being, Brian R. Little

The Acorn Principle, Jim Cathcart

What You're Really Meant To Do, Robert Steven Kaplan

One Big Thing, Phil Cooke

Practical Genius, Gina Amaro Rudan

Succeed On Your Own Terms, Hank Greenberg and Patrick Sweeney

Liberating Everyday Genius, Mary-Elaine Jacobsen

Myers-Briggs Family

www.type-Coach.com

www.myersbriggs.org

Gifts Differing, Isabel Briggs Myers with Peter B. Myers

Katherine and Isabel, Frances Wright Saunders

Personality Type: An Owner's Manual, Lenore Thomson

Portraits of Temperament, David Keirsey

Please Understand Me, David Keirsey and Marilyn Bates

Do What You Are, Paul D. Tieger and Barbara Barron-Tieger

Type Talk at Work: How the 16 Personality Types Determine Your Success on the Job, Otto Kroeger with Janet M. Thuesen and Hile Rutledge

Multiple Intelligences & Personality Type, Dario Nardi

The Enneagram Family

The Enneagram, Helen Palmer
Bringing Out The Best In Yourself At Work, Ginger Lapid-
Bogda, Ph.D.

Job Crafting Family

Article - What Is Job Crafting and Why Does It Matter?,
Justin M. Berg, Amy Wrzesniewski and Jane Dutton
Job Crafting Exercise, Justin M. Berg, Amy Wrzesniewski
and Jane Dutton
Article - Hate Your Job? Here's How To Re-Shape It!,
Jeremy Caplan
Mind Tools – Shaping Your Job To Fit You Better, The
Mind Tools Website

Strengths in Education

Creative Schools, Ken Robinson, Ph.D. and Lou Aronica
The Element, Ken Robinson
Finding Your Element, Ken Robinson
Shop Class As Soulcraft, Matthew B. Crawford
The Math Myth And Other STEM Delusions, Andrew
Hacker
Discover Your Child's Strengths, Jennifer Fox
7 Kinds of Smart, Thomas Armstrong
Awakening Your Child's Natural Genius, Thomas Armstrong
The Multiple Intelligences of Reading and Writing,
Thomas Armstrong
Multiple Intelligences In The Classroom, Thomas Armstrong

Multiple Intelligence Approaches to Assessment, David
    Lazear
*How to Develop Your Child's Gifts and Talents During the
    Elementary Years*, RaeLynne P. Rein and Rachel Rein
Brain Based Strategies to Reach Every Learner, J. Diane
    Connell
Talented Teenagers: The Roots of Success and Failure,
    Mihaly Csikszentmihalyi, Kevin Rathunde, Samuel Whalen

Strengths Development

Talent Is Never Enough, John C. Maxwell
How Successful People Grow, John C. Maxwell
The Slight Edge, Jeff Olson
*The Compound Effect: Jumpstart Your Income, Your
    Life, Your Success*, Darren Hardy
Mastery, George Leonard
*Secrets of a Buccaneer Scholar: How Self Education
    and the Pursuit of Passion Can Lead to a Lifetime
    of Success*, James Marcus Bach
*Learning As A Way Of Being: Strategies for Survival
    in a World of Permanent White Water*, Peter B. Vaill
Mindset: The New Psychology of Success, Carol S.
    Dweck, Ph.D.

Success Movement Books

The Success Principles, Jack Canfield
See You At The Top, Zig Ziglar
Lead the Field CD Series, Earl Nightingale
Unlimited Power, Anthony Robbins

Awaken The Giant Within, Anthony Robbins
Psychology of Achievement CD Series, Brian Tracy
8 To Be Great, Richard St. John
Move Ahead With Possibility Thinking, Dr. Robert Schuller
The Psychology of Winning, Dr. Denis Waitley
The Winner's Edge, Dr. Denis Waitley
University of Success, Og Mandino
Think and Grow Rich, Napoleon Hill
How to Win Friends and Influence People, Dale Carnegie

Strengths Based Goal Setting

The Right Mountain, Jim Hayhurst, Sr.
Stop Setting Goals... If You'd Rather Solve Problems,
    Bobb Biehl
Article - Follow Your River, Earl Nightingale

Strengths Based Parables

Animals Inc., Kenneth A. Tucker
*Kingdomality: An Ingenious New Way to Triumph in
    Management*, Sheldon Bowles, Richard Silvano and
    Susan Silvano
The Angel Inside, Chris Widener

Strengths and Business Leadership

The Effective Executive, Peter Drucker
Managing Oneself, Peter Drucker
Organizing Genius, Warren Bennis
Talent, Tom Peters

Good To Great, Jim Collins

Winning, Jack and Suzy Welch

Multipliers: How The Best Leaders Make Everyone Smarter, Liz Wiseman

The Ten Faces of Innovation, Tom Kelly

Shine, Edward Hallowell

Working Together: Why Great Partnerships Succeed, Michael Eisner with Aaron Cohen

Team Genius: The New Science of High-Performing Teams, Rich Karlgaard and Michael S. Malone

Surrounded by Geniuses: Unlocking the Brilliance in Yourself, Your Colleagues and Your Organization, Dr. Alan S. Gregerman

Collaborative Intelligence: Thinking with People Who Think Differently, *Dawna Markova*, Ph.D. and Angie McArthur

Powers Of Two: Finding the Essence of Innovation in Creative Pairs, Joshua Wolf Shenk

Strengths Based Selection and Hiring

The Strong Manager Program, The Marcus Buckingham Company

Getting the People Equation Right: How to Get the Right People in the Right Jobs and Keep Them, Logan Loomis

Talent Rules, Lou Adler

The Talent Solution, Edward L. Gubman

Sports Strengths

The Sports Gene, David Epstein

Cracking the Code: The Winning Ryder Cup Strategy-Making It Work for You, Paul Azinger and Dr. Ron Braund

Your Key to Sports Success, Jon P. Niednagel

Brain Types, Jon P. Niednagel

Brain Types Audio Program and Workbook, Jon P. Niednagel

The Perfect Team, Multiple Writers

Sybervision: Muscle Memory Programming for Every Sport, Steven DeVore and Gregory R. Devore with Mike Michaelson

Disabilities as Strengths in Disguise, Neurodiversity

The Power of Neurodiversity, Thomas Armstrong

The Autistic Brain: Thinking Across The Spectrum, Temple Grandin and Richard Panek

Article - The Dyslexic CEO: Charles Schwab, Richard Branson, Craig McCaw, and John Chambers triumphed over America's No. 1 Learning Disorder and Your Kids Can Too, Betsy Morris in Fortune Magazine, May 2002

The Gift of Dyslexia: Why Some of the Smartest People Can't Read... and How They Can Learn, Ronald D. Davis with Eldon M. Braun

Be Different: Adventures of a Free-Range Aspergian, John Elder Robinson

The Gift of ADHD, Lara Honos-Webb

Asperger's from the Inside Out, Michael John Carley

Developing Talents: Careers for Individuals with Asperger's Syndrome and High Functioning Autism, *Temple Grandin*, Kate Duffy and Tony Attwood

How to Find Work That Works for People with Asperger Syndrome: The Ultimate Guide for Getting People With Asperger Syndrome into the Workplace (and Keeping Them There!), Gail Hawkins

NLP (Neuro-Linguistic Programing) "Meta Programs" and "Parts"

Figuring Out People, Bob G. Bodenhamer and L. Michael Hall
Wired for Success, Wendy Jago
Mindworks, Anne Linden

Children's Books and Stories

Rudolph the Red-Nosed Reindeer, Robert L. May
The Story of Ferdinand, Munro Leaf, Drawings by Robert L. Lawson
Turtle's Flying Lesson, Diane Redfield Massie
The Oak Inside the Acorn, Max Lucado
Let Rabbits Run – A Parable, *George Revis* (Google It)
My Book About Me, Dr. Seuss and Roy McKie
Harold and the Purple Crayon, Crockett Johnson

Aesop Strengths Stories

The Tortoise and the Hare
The Scorpion and the Frog
The Peacock and the Crane

The Belly and the Members
The Three Tradesmen
The Mouse and the Bull
The Bee and the Fly
The Lion and the Stag

Passion/Dream Job Family

The Dream Manager, Matthew Kelly
Making Your Dreams Come True, Marsha Wieder
Do What You Love, The Money Will Follow, Marsha Sinetar
Wishcraft, Barbara Sher
Teamworks, Barbara Sher and Annie Gottlieb
The Passion Test - The Effortless Path to Discovering Your Destiny, Janet Bray Attwood and Chris Attwood
Live The Life You Love, Barbara Sher
I Could Do Anything If I Only Knew What It Was, Barbara Sher with Barbara Smith

The Faith Family

Fulfill Your Life, Ken Van Wyk
Living Your Strengths, Albert L. Winseman, Donald O. Clifton and Curt Liesveld
Cure for the Common Life, Max Lucado
Instinct - The Power to Unleash Your Inborn Drive, T.D. Jakes
Destiny - Step Into Your Purpose, T.D. Jakes
S.H.A.P.E. - Finding and Fulfilling Your Unique Purpose For Life, Eric Rees

You've Got Style DVD, Andy Stanley and North Point Community Church in Alpharetta, Georgia

What You Do Best In The Body of Christ, Bruce Bugbee and Willow Creek Community Church

Soul Print: Discovering Your Divine Destiny, Mark Batterson and National Community Church

Destiny Finder, Michael Brodeur

What's Your God Language?, Dr. Myra Perrine

The Three Colors of Ministry, Christian A. Schwarz

Discovering Your Ministry Identity, Paul R. Ford

Your Spiritual Gift Can Help Your Church Grow, Peter C. Wagner

Why Your Calling Is Critical CD, Tony Evans

Extraordinary, John Bevere

Soulprint, Mark Batterson

The Cause Within You, Matthew Barnett

For This I Was Born, Brian Houston

Recognizing Your Potential, Dr. Myles Munroe

Releasing Your Potential, Dr. Myles Munroe

Maximizing Your Potential, Dr. Myles Munroe

Discover Who You Are, Jane A.G. Kise, David Stark and Sandra Krebs Hirsh

Developing Your S.H.A.P.E. To Serve Others DVD, featuring Bruce Wilkinson, Joe Stowell and Carol Kent

Wired That Way, Marita Littauer and Florence Littauer

The Law of Recognition, Mike Murdock

Get A Life, Reggie McNeal

How to Deal with Annoying People, Bob Phillips and Kimberly Alyn

The Seer, Jim W. Goll

Dollars - Making Your Strengths Pay

Getting Rich Your Own Way, Srully Blotnick
The Art of Money Getting, P.T. Barnum
The Millionaire Next Door, Thomas J. Stanley and William D. Danko
The Millionaire Mind, Thomas J. Stanley and William D. Danko
Obliquity, John Kay
Purple Cow, Seth Godin
Linchpin, Seth Godin
Getting Everything You Can Out Of All You've Got, Jay Abraham
Your Secret Wealth, Jay Abraham
Differentiate or Die, Jack Trout
Positioning: The Battle for Your Mind, Ries and Trout
Compete, Byron Reeves and J. Leighton Read
Hidden Marketing Assets, Richard Johnson

The Science Behind Strengths

Frames of Mind: The Theory of Multiple Intelligences, Howard Gardner
Multiple Intelligences, Howard Gardner
The Sports Gene, David Epstein
The Blank Slate: The Modern Denial of Human Nature, Steven Pinker
Born That Way: Genes | Behavior | Personality, William Wright
You Are Extraordinary, Roger J. Williams
The Biology of Success, Dr. Bob Arnot

Biographies and Auto-Biographies

Gifted Hands: The Ben Carson Story, Ben Carson with Cecil Murphey

Creativity, Inc., Ed Catmull with Amy Wallace

The Snowball: Warren Buffett and the Business of Life, Alice Schroeder

Steve Jobs, Walter Isaacson

Einstein: His Life and Universe, Walter Isaacson

Copy This!, Paul Orfalea as told to Ann Marsh

Daily Rituals: How Artists Work, Mason Curry

It Worked For Me: In Life and Leadership, Colin Powell with Tony Koltz

Eleven Rings, Phil Jackson and Hugh Delehanty

Inside Steve's Brain, Leander Kahney

Sports Leaders and Success: 55 Top Sports Leaders and How They Achieved Greatness, Investor's Business Daily

Business Leaders and Success: 55 Top Business Leaders and How They Achieved Greatness, Investor's Business Daily

Military and Political Leaders and Success: 55 Top Military and Political Leaders and How They Achieved Greatness, Investor's Business Daily

Drucker & Me: What a Texas Entrepreneur Learned from the Father of Modern Management, Bob Buford

The Score Takes Care Of Itself, Bill Walsh with Steve Jamison and Craig Walsh

STRENGTHS DEFINITIONS

Contribution (Result, Benefit, Added Value, Difference Maker, Helpfulness, Significance, Deliverables, Profit, Performance, Solutions) Contribution is what you provide that helps attain an end result. It's the positive change that happens when you walk in the room, when you join a business unit, team or organization.

Passion (Intense Interests, Enthusiasm, Desire, Ambition, Love, Fascinations, Magnificent Obsession, Energy, Excitement) Passions are activities and subjects that make you feel strong. They may include willingness to sacrifice and suffer.

Talent (Natural Ability, Aptitude, Gift, Knack, Flair, Bent, Instinct, Genius, Inclination, Brilliance, Forte, Aptness) Talent is innate ability making performance and excellence at specific tasks easier. It also makes skill and knowledge acquisition easier with a specific domain.

Personality (Temperament, Preferences, Style, Nature, Disposition, Traits, Persona, Psyche) Personality is the organization of an individual's distinct traits and temperament.

Values (Priorities, Motivation, Beliefs, Ideals, What's Important) Values combine to build culture within an organization.

Learning Path (Perception, Organization, Retention and Response to Instruction Methods) Your learning path is your optimized pattern of acquiring and processing information.

Skills (Developed Ability, Mastery, Proficiency, Competency, Know-How, How-To including Methods, Steps, Sequences, Tool Use, Technology Use) Skills are abilities developed through deliberate systematic effort, intentional practice and often supported by training and coaching.

Knowledge (General Vocabulary, Professional Language, Industry Terminology, Rules, Regulations, Laws, Principles, Theories) Knowledge is acquired information, facts, understanding and comprehension of a subject.

Character (Honor, Morals, Ethics, Standards, Right/Wrong, Dependability, Attendance, Promptness) Character is keeping commitments, agreements and striving for excellence.

Collection - Other Strengths (Geography, Chronotype, Climate, Seasons, Pace, Spiritual Gifts, Experience, School, Bandwidth, Thinking Style, Tools, Tribe, Adversities, Disabilities) A strength is any resource, internal or external that can be turned into a marketplace contribution.

STRENGTHS SUMMARY

Contribution		
Passion	**Talents**	**Personality**
Values	**Learning Style**	**Skills**
Knowledge	**Character**	**Collection**

Printed in the United States
By Bookmasters